REBEL WOMEN

Achievements Beyond the Ordinary

LINDA KUPECEK

VICTORIA · VANCOUVER · CALGARY

Heritage House Publishing Company Ltd.
heritagehouse.ca

Library and Archives Canada Cataloguing in Publication
Kupecek, Linda
    Rebel women: achievements beyond the ordinary / Linda Kupecek. —1st Heritage House ed.

Includes bibliographical references.
ISBN 978-1-926613-75-8

    1. Women—Canada, Western—Biography. 2. Canada, Western—Biography. I. Title.

FC3208.K86 2010 .   971.2009'9   C2010-904735-4

Parts of this book originally published 2003 by Altitude Publishing Canada Ltd.

Series editor: Lesley Reynolds.
Cover design: Chyla Cardinal. Interior design: Frances Hunter.
Cover photo: Katherine Stinson and her airplane, 1916. Glenbow Archives NA-63-16. Author photo by Bill Vauthrin.

The interior of this book was produced using 100% post-consumer recycled paper, processed chlorine free and printed with vegetable-based inks.

We acknowledge the financial support of the Government of Canada through the Canada Book Fund (CBF) and the Canada Council of the Arts, and the Province of British Columbia through the British Columbia Arts Council and the Book Publishing Tax Credit.

  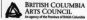

20 19 18 17   2 3 4 5
Printed in Canada

To my mother, Julia

Contents

Prologue

"HAVE YOU ORDERED THE FUEL *for the winter?" he asked.*

"What do you mean?" Georgina replied, aghast. After a difficult year farming alone, she was running out of money. She couldn't possibly afford to hire anybody to cut wood for fuel. She had assumed Wilton, the caretaker, would do it.

"The neighbours tell me I shall require 17 loads," Wilton said smugly.

"Do they!" replied Georgina forcefully. "I don't see you felling, cleaning and hauling 17 loads of wood in 17 centuries of Sundays."

They argued back and forth. Finally he delivered the incendiary statement. "You can't be expected to understand a man's duty to his family," he said solemnly.

Georgina breathed deeply. She was a single woman struggling with innumerable challenges and meeting every one, thank you very much. She stalked off and found her household hatchet, then marched into the woods. Georgina had never cut a load of wood before in her life, but anger and her so-called caretaker's complacent superiority spurred her on. To begin with, she struggled, cutting down only 12 trees in the first hour, but "gradually the work got into my blood and I liked it." Soon, she had 60 poles of wood neatly stacked.

She worked for two days, armed only with her little hatchet. But she no longer railed against Wilton. Gradually, her anger was replaced by the efforts of hard labour and the satisfaction she felt in the achievement.

The next day, Wilton announced he and his wife would walk to town. They were leaving Georgina's employ because, he said pointedly, there was no fuel for the winter.

There was a moment of silence as they stared at each other.

Then Georgina said pleasantly, "Take the wagon, only it must go out first to haul in the load of wood." After the flabbergasted Wilton returned, she said sweetly, "There are two more [wood piles] beyond. Try to get them in tomorrow." His jaw dropped even lower. In Georgina's words, Wilton and his wife "looked at each other, and at the wood, and at me, and I tried to look as unlike a person crowned with unusual honours as possible."

Mr. Wilton stayed on. How could he argue with a woman like Georgina?

1

Introduction

HISTORICALLY, WOMEN WERE PRESSURED TO play defined roles. Men were as well, but generally the roles expected of women before the feminist movement of the mid-20th century were more constricting. In Victorian times, particularly, a woman was seen as the gentle helpmate, the mother, the wife, or if employed in any career at all, as the nurse or the teacher, which were considered daring in those times. For the less privileged, there were more work opportunities: maids, cooks, servants and purveyors of pleasure.

Today, young women have options—a tremendous range of opportunities and adventures. We may rail about sexist conventions, but compared to the world 100 years ago, we live a relatively unfettered life. A century ago, a woman who dared to break from the bonds of family and marriage risked not only her inheritance, acceptance and the safety of a conventional married life, but also the ability to live without the scorn of her contemporaries. To choose a life that was outside the norm was a decision for which one could pay dearly in both material and spiritual ways.

There are many women who are rebels—celebrated women who have attained posthumous stature in Canadian history because of their political and artistic achievements. The Famous Five are no longer anonymous. Emily Carr has a cult following. So does Pauline Johnson. The more we learn about these rebel goddesses, the more we discover other, lesser-known rebels, who have also earned their place in the history of the West. Not because they created groundbreaking legislation, but because they did the unthinkable for their time: they followed their own path.

The powerful women depicted in this book, whether lovable, likeable, outrageous or sympathetic, are above all admirable for the individuality of their lives. It is sometimes said that so much of what we are is stripped away from us, day after day, year after year, by a society that often demands we take the safest and most comfortable route. As we grow older, male or female, we eventually find our way back to being who we really are.

Is there a price? Nell Shipman was overlooked because she was not as acquiescent as required; she opened an independent production company just when the major

Introduction

Hollywood studios began exerting their power. Isabel Gunn, once discovered as a woman, lost her livelihood and her respectability. Almost everyone universally scorned Mother Fulham. Georgina Binnie-Clark railed against unjust laws. Yet each managed to find the strength to be who she was in spite of the costs.

In *Rebel Women*, we discover women who had the courage to flout convention and follow their hearts, despite conflict, pain, adversity and doubt. They have all left their mark in the history of western Canada.

2

Nell Shipman
(1892–1970)

I did not like the way they dressed their contract players. This was in the period of curly blondes with Cupid's bow mouths; and . . . yards of floaty gauze at the waistline . . . This long-legged, lanky, outdoors gal, who usually loped across the Silver Screen in fur parkas and mukluks, simply gagged at such costuming. And had the nerve to refuse it."

—NELL SHIPMAN, ON TURNING DOWN
A SEVEN-YEAR CONTRACT WITH SAM GOLDWYN

NELL SHIPMAN HAD MORE THAN NERVE. She had talent and true grit. In 1919, the silent-screen star and a film crew travelled to Lesser Slave Lake in northern Alberta to shoot a movie. Nell was the writer, leading performer and creative genius of the film. The shoot of *Back to God's Country* was horrific in every way: shockingly cold temperatures, primitive living conditions and creative and personal conflicts. Yet under Nell's creative control, the film survived the forces of nature and the flaws of human beings. Unlike most other silent movies of the time, it featured a strong, active heroine, sympathetic filming of animals and one of the first (and very tasteful) nude scenes on film. It was also one of the huge commercial successes of the era.

Nell was born Helen Barham in 1892, in Victoria, British Columbia. Her father was a remittance man and her mother a gentlewoman. Nell grew up in a home filled with crested silver, fine china and music. She was on the path to a conventional life as a wife and helpmate, but from the time Nell had seen her first pantomime as a seven-year-old in London, England, she wanted to be on the stage. Nothing could stop her.

At the age of 13, Nell left home to work. She abandoned the opportunity of education and a possible musical career as a pianist to become what was at the time a shocking thing indeed—an actress! As Nell wrote years later, she was "not a Mrs. Siddons or Ellen Terry but a shabby little tramp of a backwoods trouper in a one-night-stand Company." Her life on the road, from Seattle to Alaska to New York with myriad stops in between, was every mother's worst nightmare: cancelled tours, cheap hotels and unsavoury companions. Nell was feisty and ambitious, but also naive. During this period, she suffered from recurrent nightmares. "I had begun the long traumatic trail which ultimately led me to a mental, physical and spiritual distrust of human beings balanced by a love for animals which was to dominate my life." Nell's mother, Rose, was an unlikely stage mother, but despite her distaste for the vulgar life of vaudeville, she became for a while her daughter's companion and protector on the rocky road to fame.

By her 18th birthday, Nell was back in Seattle, where her parents had settled. She feared she had failed miserably as an actress. Seeking work, but expecting none, Nell knocked on the door of the Third Avenue Theatre in Seattle. There she met a blond businessman with blue eyes and a wide grin. His name was Ernest Shipman.

A theatrical entrepreneur, Ernie had an eye for the dollars and the ladies. According to Nell, "He had the bounce of a rubber ball, the buoyancy of a balloon, though the first can wear out under hard usage and the last suffer ill winds and the prick of evil fortune. He was one of the great cocksmen of his time, not immoral but amoral, not lascivious but lusty." He was known as "Ten Per Cent Ernie" because of his custom of retaining 10 per cent of the wages of his employees. Eighteen-year-old Nell married the 31-year-old Ernie and became the fourth Mrs. Shipman, a relationship that lasted seven years.

Nell's career blossomed under Ernie's guidance and ambition. He was a master promoter, and the newly married couple embarked on a series of theatrical tours. They eventually settled in Los Angeles, where Ernie felt they could cash in on the flourishing motion-picture industry.

And they did. A combination of Ernie's salesmanship and Nell's acting and writing talents put them on the map as film professionals. Even when temporarily sidelined by her pregnancy with son Barry, Nell regularly churned out two-reelers that established her credibility as a scriptwriter. They were on a roll: Nell was in demand as a writer, most notably for adaptations of the works of outdoor writer James Oliver Curwood, and Ernie was capable of cooking up deals with publishers and studios, exploiting Nell's talent. Nell was also a leading lady, known for her believable performances in rugged outdoor pictures, in which she often performed her own stunts.

Cinematographer Joseph Walker remembers meeting her for the first time: "Nell Shipman was the true prototype of the outdoors woman. Handsome, well-proportioned and tall, with melting brown eyes and a thick mass of long dark hair coiled around her head, she knew exactly what she wanted, but at the same time, she was warmly feminine." When Joseph Walker shot a screen test of her, Nell insisted it be outdoors in bright sunlight with natural settings. She wanted the direct opposite of the usual perfectly lit artificial settings.

It was a rough and tumble film world in those days. The shooting of a motion picture was a collaborative effort, which meant there was tremendous creative commitment but few safety precautions for performers and crew. During the filming of *A Gentleman's Agreement* in 1917 (not to be confused with the later film of the same title), Nell battled the currents of a river on camera, when, not as planned, she suddenly had to rescue the leading man from drowning. In another incident, the crew abandoned Nell in a hospital following an exhausting water scene when she collapsed "cold as a mackerel." She climbed out the hospital-room window and drove her Cadillac roadster home.

Nell and Ernie formed a partnership with James Oliver Curwood, who had written many of the stories on which Nell's stardom had been launched. Their next project was ambitious. Nell was a star, Ernie a brilliant promoter and Curwood was a famous author. They formed the Shipman-Curwood Motion Picture Production Company in November of 1918 and started to plan their first project together, a film called *Back to God's Country*. But as they were preparing for the production, Spanish influenza struck, the first bad omen. Nell was one of the victims and fell into a coma. When she awakened, her beloved mother had died, taken by the same illness.

Yet the show must go on. Nell, Ernie, cinematographer Joseph Walker and the crew of *Back to God's Country* boarded a train for Calgary. In January 1919, the *Calgary Herald* announced Ernest Shipman's arrival in Calgary to address the city's board of trade. In reality, Ernie was in Calgary to pitch the potential returns of investing in the film industry. He hoped to raise money to produce *Back to God's Country*. Nell's presence at the Palliser Hotel created a flurry of newspaper articles predicting that Calgary would soon become the centre of the motion-picture industry in North America.

The publicity was effective. Canadian Photoplays Ltd. was incorporated on February 17, 1919, with a capitalization of $250,000. *Back to God's Country* was to be the first production of many. Shares sold at $100 each to an enthusiastic response from the Calgary business community.

Nell and Curwood met for the first time in Calgary at the elegant Palliser Hotel, one of the grand dames of the Canadian Pacific Railway chain. He lambasted her script and insisted on changes that supported his original he-man story, "Wapi, the Walrus," but conflicted with her sensibility. She was committed to a vision of a world in which humans and animals coexisted in harmony and women were active protagonists. He wanted more feral fare. In his rendition of the woodland nude scene, "the Girl did not simply look at the man who would rape her as she came naked from a forest pool. She trembled. Her fluttering hands clothed her heaving bosom, tears, like spilled opals, coursed her pale cheeks and her hair, her bountiful, glorious hair, glistened wet from her swim with her pet bear and flowed about her alabaster shoulders like a protective mantle." Ernie urged Nell to agree with Curwood's changes to avoid rocking the boat. She willingly placated the great author, knowing she could rewrite on location. "Wapi, the Walrus all the way!" she wrote in her autobiography. "What we'd sneak in as human drama after Curwood was safely back [home] was my affair."

On March 10, Nell and the company were feted at a luncheon in Calgary. Soon after, Nell, Walker, production manager Bert Van Tuyle and the cast and crew travelled north by train. Ernie stayed in Calgary to finalize the all-important money matters.

The film was shot on location on the shores of Lesser Slave Lake, 260 kilometres north of Edmonton. The outrageously severe location was determined by several factors: Canadian investment, which required the film be shot in Canada; Curwood's contract, which guaranteed that he pick the locations; and the requirement of a frozen lake for some of the scenes.

At the deserted community of Faust, the cast and crew jumped off the train into the snow and were met by dog teams. They were warned not to breathe deeply, as the extremely cold air could freeze their lungs, and told never to wear leather shoes outdoors, as severe frostbite could result. Both warnings were unheeded, with severe consequences.

Ferocious winter storms blowing off the lake and extreme temperatures of −50°C greeted the film crew and stars. The crew's accommodations consisted of abandoned fisherman's shacks and a cookhouse on the shore of the lake, all under a blanket of snow. Only two cabins had stoves. One was assigned to Nell, the other to Curwood and his wife, who, after a few days in the arctic cold, leaped on the next train back to civilization. Nell assigned their vacated cabin to leading man Ronald Byram.

From this inauspicious beginning, the shoot was marked by "obstacles unprecedented and trouble never dreamed of," according to Ernie. Most of the crew fled after only a few days in the freezing temperatures, leaving Van Tuyle to complete the carpentry work himself. The cheery company press releases of the time, however, mentioned only minor inconveniences. An announcement was made that the leading man was suffering from a "severe cold," when in fact Ronald Byram was gravely ill. According to Walker's recollections, after drinking too much, Byram had staggered out into the freezing air and had unwisely shown his defiance of the weather by breathing deeply. They rushed him by dogsled and train to an Edmonton hospital, where he died of pneumonia. Quickly and quietly, the production replaced him with another actor. This wasn't the only disaster to befall the shoot. Bert Van Tuyle, wearing leather shoes, incurred a severe case of frostbite through his efforts building a ship on the lake or his work one day on camera as a sled driver. This affliction would haunt him for years.

Under these extreme conditions, emotions ran close to the surface. Marooned in the wilderness, in a tremendously difficult position, Nell led a cast and crew in unspeakable conditions. Yet her indomitable spirit prevailed. Throughout the film, the character of Dolores is strong and courageous. The same was true of Nell in real life.

In a key scene in the film, Nell (as the character Dolores) intervenes in the beating of a vicious dog. Her co-stars were two Great Danes: Rex, the gentle dog, and Tresore, a vicious dog who reportedly attacked everything and everybody in sight. There are several versions of what happened next. Either Nell had already befriended Tresore before the scene or, as Joseph Walker remembers, she did the unbelievable. As the cameras rolled, Nell walked into the scene and threw her arms around Tresore before the dogs were switched, as was the norm. "We stood horrified. Nobody dared speak," recalls Walker. The killer dog looked her in the eye and then lowered his head. She had tamed him. Moments later, the second cameraman, thinking the dog was gentle, approached him. Tresore lunged and bit the camera tripod in two.

Van Tuyle lost control. "What a damned fool thing to do!" he shouted at Nell.

"I've already told you—I knew I'd be all right. I just knew. But don't ask me how I knew," she replied.

Then they looked into each other's eyes with electrifying intensity. Ernie, the charming scoundrel, was no longer the main man in Nell's life. Van Tuyle and Nell had found love in northern Alberta.

By the time the two-week shoot in Lesser Slave Lake ended, the overjoyed cast and what remained of the crew caught the next train south to continue filming in California. But a desperate pall hung over them. Bert Van Tuyle, the

Nell Shipman was well known for her empathy and harmony with animals and the wilderness. BOISE STATE UNIVERSITY LIBRARY, NELL SHIPMAN COLLECTION

film's production manager and Nell's new beau, had disappeared. Crazed by the thought of the possible amputation of his foot due to the frostbite he had suffered, he reportedly was en route to San Francisco to drink away the pain.

How was Nell to continue?

Things turned worse before they got better. In Calgary, Ernie greeted her with the news of her father's death. Nell had lost her mother, her brother had been gassed in the First World War and now her father had died. Nell was adamant that work had to go on. She continued south to California; the shoot was far from over.

The much-publicized nude scene in *Back to God's Country* was filmed impromptu at Kern River in California. At first, Nell was to wear a body stocking, but because it wrinkled distastefully when wet, she decided to do the scene nude, choosing the camera angles carefully with the cinematographer. The result is one of the most striking and elegant scenes in the film. There is no awkwardness, no feeling of exploitation or discomfort. It is a playful scene co-starring a tamed bear and is a tremendous tribute to Nell's empathy with animals and the wilderness. It is also a reminder to filmmakers today how joyful and life-affirming bare skin can be.

Nell is no shrinking violet in this film. She was known for doing her own stunts and for her growing love of animals. *Back to God's Country* featured several animal co-stars, including Nell's favourite, a bear named Big Brownie. Nell was determined to direct her animal cast without whips, shouts, probes or drugs. "Now I was acting with a free, large bear who might bite, hug or merely swat. She reared, put an arm about my waist, drew me close, gave me a tentative sniff, then licked my cheek, pushed me gently aside and dropped to the ground at my feet. While I relaxed in her embrace I knew my theory was okay, and that it was a fifty-fifty deal between human and animals . . . All about us and within us was serene, untroubled, unquestioned. No personal bravery in this, just the fact of communication."

Nell had the courage to defy film studios and to maintain her own vision in her works. One of the loveliest scenes in *Back to God's Country* was the result of her imaginative mind: "In *Back to God's Country* . . . sitting on the floor, leaning against a large plain door of dark wood, I was to dream of my Northwoods home and my wild animal friends. The lensman genius, Joe Walker, went along with my notion. I claimed that people did not dream clean-cut, single visions but mixtures. I wanted the wilderness inhabitants to blend in and out, here a wolf, there a bear, over in a tree a cougar, a raccoon washing his dinner in a stream, squirrels popping in and out, bobcats peering, porcupines bristling, all of them dissolving in a montage while I, at the bottom of the frame, dreamed it. It was the most difficult double exposure ever attempted." When *Back to God's Country* was released, the reviews praised "some of the most remarkable animal stuff ever photographed." Nell's empathy and harmony with nature and animals was evident. She had no fear.

The distributor First National released the film in September 1919 to rave reviews, particularly for Nell and her interaction with her animal co-stars. Nell's love of animals had paid off for her, creatively and professionally. The film grossed over a half-million dollars in the first year, a 300 per cent return to its Calgary investors and an amazing feat for the time.

Despite the huge success of *Back to God's Country*, Nell and Ernie divorced shortly afterward. There may have been several reasons for the split: perhaps Ernie, now in his forties, was jealous of 27-year-old Nell's involvement with production manager Bert Van Tuyle; perhaps it was the nightmare shoot in Lesser Slave Lake; perhaps, as in many partnerships, it was simply time to part ways.

Alas, strong, independent Nell, who loved animals and men (maybe in that order), seemed to have been undone by a series of lovers who were con men and drunkards. Each saw her strength and creativity as a ticket to their success. After she and Ernie divorced, Nell moved to Priest Lake, Idaho, with Bert Van Tuyle. Here they maintained a zoo and an independent production company. Lionhead Lodge was a legend in the Northwest, a place where Nell Shipman and her entourage of animals made movies. But Bert, now a drunkard, suffered recurrent problems with the frostbite he had endured at Lesser Slave Lake. Their isolated home was a challenge in winter. Bert once wandered off, delirious with the gangrene that was a legacy of his frostbite, and Nell, in a replay of a pivotal scene in *Back to God's Country*, had to rescue him. He staggered off into the cold, and she followed with a dog team. He was insane and threatening, simultaneously homicidal and suicidal, but she loved him and was determined to save his life. And she did.

Nell began to view herself as a woman who "sometimes

Part of the poster for *Back to God's Country.* GLENBOW ARCHIVES NA-1273-1

made moving pictures." When she tried to sell *Trail of the Northwind,* a two-reeler about animals and humans overcoming obstacles together, the Pathe Company had no interest. There was no villain. And no sex. "I wondered if audiences would not enjoy a respite from sexpot pursuit."

Nell had more success selling her screenplays, including *Wings in the Dark* (1935), starring Cary Grant and Myrna Loy, which was reportedly the first film about a seeing-eye dog. Yet much of her time was spent dodging creditors. Eventually, her menagerie of animals was consigned to the San Diego Zoo, as she could no longer afford their upkeep. In 1963, destitute and at her wit's end, she applied to the Motion Picture Relief Fund for assistance, sending them her resumé. Her request was refused. She was informed her credits were not recent enough to qualify.

Nell never ceased to pursue creative projects, whether they were screenplays, books or plays. As an artist, she created milestones in cinema. She had more to say and do, yet she was denied the opportunity. She once said, "Applause and Recognition are the Handmaidens of Creativity." Yet despite the lack of these in her later years, she was incredibly productive. She died in 1970, shortly after completing her autobiography, *The Silent Screen and My Talking Heart.*

Although she had four husbands in all, she spent her last years single, still striving for expression as an artist and still defiantly independent. "And don't let anyone suggest that perhaps 'Nell will return to the fold and all will be as it once was and should be, world everlasting, if we are all married to each other and everything is all set and clean and tidy'. Because I won't. I will never be married again to anyone," she wrote in 1933.

Nell was a true independent, creating an image of women vastly different from the usual onscreen delicate flower. She had tremendous creative control. She presented a view of nature and of women that was dismissed by the Hollywood powers. She ran an independent production company when the big studios were gaining power, and this was her downfall. The studios punished her independent spirit. Tragically, her vibrant, joyful voice was muted. The last words in her autobiography are:

> There they go
> Free from woe
> Forgetting me
> Aw, Gee!

Yet Nell lives on. Her cinematic legacy has been restored, most notably by the National Archives of Canada and Boise State University. Books, articles and websites abound. Nell succeeded in creating works of art that expressed a strong feminine perspective, a humanist point of view, a love of animals and her enduring strength of character. Her rebellious, unquenchable spirit lives forever in her films.

3

Flores LaDue
(1883–1951)

"Address: The World" —FLORES LADUE

YOUNG GRACE MAUD BENSELL DID what many children yearned to do in the early 1900s. She ran away to join the circus, resourcefully sweeping away her tracks in the snow so she couldn't be caught and hauled back to the family home. And she never was. Instead, she changed her name to Flores LaDue and followed her gypsy heart, making a career as a hugely successful rodeo performer and vaudevillian in what had been a man's world. No demure little curtsies for Flores. She rode, she roped, she astounded. She became the Champion Lady Fancy Roper of the World.

Grace was born in 1883 in Montevideo, Minnesota, into a

privileged life as the daughter of Charles Bensell, a prominent lawyer who later became a judge. She started riding horses on her father's ranches when she was four years old, becoming an accomplished rider and roper. As a very young woman, she escaped the constraints of a traditional life and her widowed father's disapproval of her cowgirl dreams and found a job with a travelling circus. Then she joined Col. Fred T. Cummins Wild West and Indian Congress. Grace burst out of her conservative background to become Flores LaDue. She worked the rodeo circuits, Wild West shows and John P. Kirk's Elite Vaudeville Company, becoming a skilled trick roper.

Flores LaDue was tiny and dark haired, with flashing eyes and incredible agility. Even to modern eyes, the vintage photos of Flores are amazing. They show her hanging upside down from a horse while twirling a lariat or lying on the ground spinning a giant circle of rope over her head. To audience members in the early 20th century, she must have seemed like a magic act.

LaDue constantly attracted attention, but she especially caught the eye of the irrepressible and dashing Guy Weadick, another trick roper, who was eventually the force behind the creation of the famous Calgary Stampede. Weadick was a tall, slim cowboy with the gift of the gab and boundless energy. Judging from his photos, he was a handsome man, with grace and flamboyant style in the western way. Guy and Flores met in 1906 during Col. Fred T. Cummins Wild West and Indian Congress. They were married five

Flores LaDue, World Champion Trick and Fancy Roper.

weeks later in Memphis, Tennessee. She was 23; he was 21. From then on, they were a team, but one in which she was an equal and skilled partner, not the helpmate most women were expected to be upon marriage.

Together, Flores LaDue and Guy Weadick were a powerful force as a much-in-demand trick and fancy roping vaudeville team who toured with western personality Will Rogers and bulldogger Bill Pickett. They appeared on Broadway in rodeo-themed shows like *Billy the Kid* and toured the world, from St. Petersburg to South America. The period from 1910 to 1920 was the golden age of vaudeville, and Guy Weadick and Flores LaDue were riding high.

Weadick was not only a cowboy and trick roper, but also a fabulous showman. Guy and Flores bantered throughout their 15-minute act while performing deeds that made the crowds gasp. According to a newspaper account of the time, as quoted in *The Papers of Will Rogers*, "The woman of the team is very small, very dark complexioned and very wiry. She rides a horse like an Indian and spins the lariat with a skill that draws forth frequent applause . . . The man (Weadick) tied the woman (LaDue) up completely by circling her legs, arms and head with the coils, and the act was finished when the woman spun a lariat from horseback. The couple do quite a little talking, which gets across nicely."

Flores, barely five feet tall, had already established herself as a fearless competitor. She was known as the first woman to perform the "Texas Skip," an intricate rope trick during which the performer leaps back and forth through a vertical loop. In *The Cowboy Spirit,* Donna Livingstone comments on this incredible skill: "Trick roping involves only the roper and the rope. It is loose-jointed free form poetry, full of humour and wit with a generosity of motion that is a delight to watch."

When the Weadicks landed in Calgary, Guy persuaded the four entrepreneurs who became known as the Big Four (George Lane, Patrick Burns, A.E. Cross and Archie McLean) to fund the first Calgary Stampede in 1912. The event, now an internationally known tourist attraction, was intended as a tribute to the Old West, with a rodeo competition as its key component. Flores won the title of World Champion Trick and Fancy Roper in an intense match with another star cowgirl, Lucille Mulhall. Particularly impressive was Flores' ability to tie a double hitch in the rope with only two movements of her wrist.

One of the unusual aspects of this first Calgary Stampede was Weadick's willingness to make female rodeo competitors as visible and as honoured as the male contestants. It may have been his eagerness to give his wife the superstar recognition she warranted (although she certainly was not wanting in this area) or it may have been that his marriage to an international rodeo star made him appreciate the commercial appeal of daring cowgirls.

The journalists of the day, previously not known for their coverage of women's news, other than fashion notes, devoted much space to the women's competitive events. The Glenbow Museum Archives and many fine books on female rodeo competitors illustrate how striking and confident these early women rodeo competitors were. Thanks to the coverage in Calgary, Flores and other top cowgirls, such as Tillie Baldwin and Bertha Blancett, continued to get extensive attention from the press at other rodeos, including the 1912 New York Stampede.

Today we take the prowess of female athletes for granted, but in the early 1900s, people were astounded by these women who performed courageous deeds with horses, ropes and steers while wearing daring clothing, such as divided skirts and pantaloons. At first, crowds didn't know what to make of it, but then they applauded wildly. In Montana, a competitive cowgirl was threatened with arrest for riding into town wearing a divided skirt. Yet it was necessary for female competitors to find clothing that allowed them to move freely as athletes while preserving their modesty. A long and trailing skirt would not only look foolish, it would be suicidal.

Flores LaDue, along with her colleagues on the Wild West–show circuit, blazed the trail to make women a vital part of professional rodeo. It seems a wild and wonderful life, performing to applause, doing what has not been done before, but there was also hardship in touring and taking on the unknown.

According to Mary Lou LeCompte in *Cowgirls of the Rodeo,*

pioneer cowgirls like Flores and her contemporaries "helped make women's contests an integral part of professional rodeo . . . They demonstrated that females were capable of far greater physical achievements than was generally believed possible . . . It was not an easy life and many women did drop out due to lack or money or loss of desire. Those who remained, reveled in the excitement of travel, bright lights and the thrill of competition."

In *The Cowboy Spirit*, Weadick biographer Donna Livingstone outlines the rigours of touring, playing two to three theatres a week with two to three performances a day, whether the stop was New York or one of the Canadian cities on what was known as "The Death Trail" because of the cold weather and small theatres. It wasn't all dreary, as Livingstone notes: "There were advantages, however, to the northern circuit. Prohibition was still in effect in the United States, but Canada wasn't yet 'dry', and it warmed the heart of many a vaudevillian to see the fine array of whiskey on store shelves."

Weadick, with Flores' support, had made a huge success of the first Calgary Stampede. Flores didn't do too badly herself, as it was a venue in which she was able to compete and triumph. It would be a few years before the next Calgary Stampede, so Weadick promoted shows elsewhere, and they continued their vaudeville act.

In 1920, they bought a ranch in Longview, near High River, Alberta, where the foothills, the mountains, the

Flores LaDue performs a fancy rope trick at the Calgary Stampede. It is likely that this photograph was taken at the first ever Calgary Stampede in 1912. GLENBOW ARCHIVES NA-628-4

untouched air and the blue skies combined to make a perfect retirement spot. They hadn't retired yet, though. Weadick and LaDue worked the vaudeville circuit during the winter and maintained the Stampede Ranch the rest of the year. They carefully avoided calling it a dude ranch, even though it was clearly a moneymaking enterprise for two vaudevillians and show people who knew how appealing a safe rendezvous with the Wild West would be to rich city folk. The brochures were effusive, aimed at advertising a guest-ranch environment.

They installed amenities that were advanced for the day, including an indoor toilet, running water and a shelved food cooler that lowered into the ground.

As vaudeville faded in the late 1920s, the two stars faced challenging times. Flores ran the business part of the ranch and was apparently a tough boss, demanding much of her hired hands and making sure the wranglers were dressed appropriately and the horses were treated well. Weadick handled the charm, sales and drinking department, wooing potential customers while trying to drum up work for either himself or the duo. According to some sources, Flores, ever enterprising, maintained a successful sideline trading in uncut diamonds. She wore a pouch of stones around her neck, selling and buying as circumstances required.

The partnership of these two icons of western Canadian history lasted for 45 years. Although there were rough spots, they remained committed to each other. But Flores was not a drooping flower. She was a vibrant, strong woman, whether on the fairgrounds or on the ranch. Apparently, Weadick's enthusiasm and outgoing nature extended to romances (or flings) outside of his marriage, and this did not sit well with Flores. Their house was decorated with gifts of penance from Weadick to LaDue, from silver candlesticks to an inlaid coffee table. Although the details are not clear, he reportedly once shared his car with another woman, and Flores was not amused. She swore she would never set foot in the vehicle again. For the next months, neighbours were entertained by the sight of the Weadicks travelling to town in two vehicles. Weadick would lead, opening the 22 gates. Flores would follow in her car and close the 22 gates. Apparently, the same routine would happen on their return.

She was not a reverent or subservient partner. She was known to shout with good humour, "For God's sake, Guy, shut up!" when his alcohol-fuelled monologues went on too long. The Stampede Ranch was the site of many parties and celebrations, including a legendary talking competition, which Weadick won, of course.

As Flores and Guy settled into their lives as guest-ranch owners, they tried to maintain their rodeo presence while exploring various ways of making money. Their ranch was the location for two early silent westerns. Universal Pictures' *The Calgary Stampede*, filmed in 1925, starred silent-film star Hoot Gibson and featured the chuckwagon races Weadick had helped make famous in the first Stampede. In 1928, *His Destiny*, an early silent western financed in part by Weadick and Calgary investors, was filmed at the ranch and in other areas of southern Alberta. Weadick played a major role, and there were cameos by well-known Calgary residents. The film, produced by British Canadian Pictures Ltd. and distributed by Paramount, was a success, yet it apparently did not bring the couple the financial security they desired.

LaDue and Weadick still ran the ranch as a team. Even though their income was reduced, the former stars made do. His flamboyance and her common sense kept them going.

The Prince of Wales, later King Edward VIII and then the Duke of Windsor, was a neighbour on the rare occasions he visited Alberta, and Flores reportedly taught him some fancy rope tricks.

By this time, Flores' father, Charles Bensell, who had forgiven her for running away to join the circus, had come to live with them. He passed away shortly after his 92nd birthday and was buried in High River.

The child Grace Maud Bensell had rebelled. She had left a safe little life with her father, a life of financial certainty with no risks, to become a gypsy. And so she did, with her Wild West husband and her Wild West ways. She dazzled the world with her undisputed rodeo skills. She and Weadick roamed the world as entertainers and athletes and made their mark as rodeo royalty, vaudeville stars and key players in the establishment of what is now known as the greatest outdoor rodeo show in the world.

When Flores' health began to fail, they sold the ranch and bought a house in High River. As a farewell note in the ranch guestbook, she wrote, "Flores LaDue Weadick. Address: The World." The couple then moved to Phoenix, Arizona, to escape the bitterly cold Alberta winters. At their going-away party, hundreds showed up to bid them goodbye, and they were presented with a substantial cash gift gathered from their friends and admirers. Flores LaDue died in 1951, during a return visit to High River. Weadick was heartbroken. Her headstone reads: "A True Partner."

Nobody would dispute this. She was not a submissive participant in the fame of her husband; she was famous and accomplished in her own right. She was not a trophy wife; she had her own trophies. In 2001, she was posthumously inducted into the National Cowgirl Museum and Hall of Fame in Fort Worth, Texas. The inscription on her riding saddle, a legacy to a friend in Longview, reads, "Flores LaDue World Champion Lady Fancy Roper, Calgary 1912–1919, Winnipeg 1913, New York 1915. Retired undefeated."

Perhaps this is what Flores LaDue was above all else: undefeated. Not by any rodeo competitors. Not by a straying husband. Not by the challenges of a wandering life. Her flashing eyes, so frequently described by the press, and her incredible skills as a trick roper made her memorable to audiences around the world. Her ability to adapt and run a ranch and wrangle an exuberant cowboy husband is another testimony to her inner strength.

Despite a second marriage, Weadick apparently never recovered from Flores' death. He died in 1953 and was buried next to his true partner—a vibrant woman who made her mark in the world, contributed to the success of the man she loved, but never was second fiddle.

4

Georgina Binnie-Clark (1871–1947)

"Paton, if I'd wanted to be dictated to by a man, I would have married one and let him keep me."

—GEORGINA BINNIE-CLARK,
DURING A DISPUTE WITH A HIRED HAND

IN 1905, GEORGINA BINNIE-CLARK and her sister arrived in Saskatchewan from England to visit their brother, Lal. Their intention was to check up on the state of Lal's homestead for their curious father before travelling on to New York, where Georgina planned to continue her writing career. But the two sisters discovered that their brother was an unrepentant failure at farming, and they had to spend their return fare to England trying to bail him out. They ended up stranded in Lipton, Saskatchewan. Georgina then embarked on an astounding adventure in farming, doing what few women had done before.

In Victorian England, second sons (who would not inherit unless the first son met an untimely death) were expected to seek careers in a field suitable to their class. Even though Harvey J. Philpot's *Guide Book to the Canadian Dominion Containing Full Information for the Emigrant, the Tourist, the Sportsman, and the Small Capitalist* warned against sending wastrel sons to Canada, where farm work was a necessary prerequisite, many young men were sent with the fervent hope that they would either make good or disappear without dishonouring the family name. Unfortunately, Lal was well on his way to becoming a major blot on the reputation of the Binnie-Clark family.

The situation for women was different. Women were expected to marry into their class. Unfortunately, the emigration of men to Canada and other countries, in addition to mortalities from England's frequent wars, left a generation of genteel unmarried women without means. There were reportedly 800,000 more women than men in Britain in 1861, and the plight of the "redundant" gentlewoman was much discussed. For a working-class woman, a lack of the male commodity was not disastrous. There were jobs in farms, factories, shops and in homes as domestic servants. But for women like Georgina and her sister, Hilaria, whose real name was Ethel, life as a single woman was more threatening. The "gentlewoman" (the siblings came from a family of sufficient means that they could be so described) was not expected to work for a living. Her success was determined by her marriage, not by her vocation. As a result, Georgina and Hilaria had precious little experience of running a household, although Hilaria was an excellent cook, and they certainly had no idea how to plough a field or when to harvest a crop of wheat. They were totally unsuited to the requirements of homesteading life.

Georgina and Hilaria did not arrive in Canada as immigrants, but as young women keen on a new experience as Edwardian tourists. Georgina, an established journalist in Britain, was hoping for work in New York. Her trip to Lipton, Saskatchewan, financed by her father, was a convenient way to get to North America. "It is the easier way to my destination. In finding out exactly what a father's capital has accomplished on a brother's homestead, I earn my fare," she wrote with the practical point of view that characterized her writings.

Or so she thought. Georgina and Hilaria travelled by train to the area near Fort Qu'Appelle, Saskatchewan, expecting that Lal (one of the British second sons sent to the colonies) and his partner, Hicks, were successful Canadian farmers. Lal greeted them at the train station with the heartfelt words: "You can form no idea of the ghastly, lonely, hateful life! The awful people! The beastly discomfort! I give you a week at the outside. Hicks gives you till your first mosquito bite."

Somewhat taken aback, Georgina and Hilaria insisted on travelling to the "homestead" Lal and Hicks had built on the prairie. What greeted them was an odd little hut that "leaned disconsolately to the right."

Lal, who would be described in contemporary terms as laid-back, or, more unkindly, a slacker, was perfectly amiable in the face of embarrassment, as recorded by Georgina in one of the books she later wrote about the experience:

"My shack has an air of its own. It's original."

"It's original," I allowed.

"Original!" mocked Hilaria. "We will hope it is unique."

The shack was a disaster, with broken plaster, the sky gleaming through the holes in the roof, a pit in the middle of the room for a cellar and two canvas stretchers for beds. Where was the glorious homestead their father had financed? Instead, they found two good-natured incompetents, who, they soon discovered, were the objects of great scorn.

Most women of Georgina's class would have flinched and left on the first train back to so-called civilization. Instead, mortified by the disdain in which their neighbours held her brother, Georgina was determined to redeem the family name. She declared to Hilaria, "Father will lose every cent he has advanced to Lal if we don't make some sort of definite effort . . . If we can only secure the ultimate possession of the land, that at least will represent something; but if you and I don't see these duties completed, they won't be done and the land grant will be cancelled."

The Canadian Homestead Act excluded most women from claiming the 160 acres (65 hectares) that were allowed as a gift to a man. Georgina resented this inequity, and during her stay in Canada, she periodically waged a battle with the government on this topic. But first there was work to be done. The claimed land had to be ploughed and seeded in three years or it would be returned to the government. The money for the fare home for herself and Hilaria was invested in an attempt to save Lal's sinking homestead.

Georgina was moved by the expanse of the country and intrigued by the opportunity in farming. "As we drove through patches of amber wheat I vowed I would not acquiesce in failure. I would make one strong straight effort to get on the line of prosperity which others seemed to find in Canada." Lal struggled on and fulfilled his homestead duties with an unforgettable lack of enthusiasm. He eventually sold the house and land for £220 and escaped to new, equally inept efforts.

Won over by the land, Georgina purchased a farm of her own near Fort Qu'Appelle, Saskatchewan, using $1,000 from her income as a guarantee for the down payment. She assumed that her father would help finance the endeavour. Shortly after, a letter from her father arrived with stern instructions: under no conditions was she to buy land. Her siblings were astounded by what they considered a rash act on Georgina's part. "Ha Ha! A woman work a Canadian farm! Why, you would be the laughing-stock of the country, if you could do it, which you can't," was Lal's response.

But she did. In England, she had never worked with her hands, not even doing household chores. In Saskatchewan, she learned to plough, feed and water horses, milk a cow and myriad other "manly" tasks. Georgina endured difficult times. She encountered prejudice against her gender, her choice to be a single woman and her determination to make a success of what seemed to many to be a quixotic leap onto the prairie. She was told again and again, "Ain't no work for a woman."

Georgina had bought the best farm in the area in terms of wheat land, but it was also the "dirtiest," filled with wild oats and French weed, also called stinkweed. She had a tremendous chore in terms of clearing and breaking her 16-hectare lot. All the while, brother Lal, from his home-stead, and sister Hilaria wailed desperately about wanting to go home. Hilaria fled as soon as possible to find work as a nurse in Winnipeg in order to finance her return to England. But there was no nursing work, and she was forced to return, furious, trailing suitors and admirers. When Georgina went to fetch her, she found Hilaria was not destitute as expected, but surrounded by jolly Canadian lads who were sorry to relinquish her to her sister's care. "It is never what Hilaria says, but always how she says it," notes Georgina. "I have yet to meet the masculine entity for whom she cannot affect a tender interest."

The daily labour was only one of Georgina's challenges. She also faced a succession of hired hands who either wouldn't work for a woman or, like her brother, wouldn't work at all. On the matter, Georgina advised that "the best system of all for the woman-farmer is to train herself to do all her own chores and hire her field labourer at special seasons by the day even if she has to pay the highest market price. In Britain we grow up with the idea that kitchens and bedrooms are born clean and remain in that state without labour: none can make clear the labour and energy which women distribute, looking after the personal needs of men who never give a thought to the work they are creating, but will spend hours meditating on the work they can evade."

One of her hired hands quit just before harvest because she hurt his feelings when she said he was slow. Quitting before harvest is a sin against a farmer, but she had to deal with it. "I was too busy to worry. I wasted no time in words, but mowed and raked and got right down to the ploughing." Another farm worker, recently out of jail, rhapsodized about the lodging and food in the Regina prison and the kindness of the institution. He didn't much care for a woman boss. The last straw for Georgina was when, after he had boasted in a blood-curdling way of his great talents as a pig butcher, she sent him and Lal to dispense with her pigs. After much drama, the two men came back shaken. The pigs had won. She was furious. Her brother and a supposedly hard-hearted and bloodthirsty convict had wilted at the sight of squealing pigs. Luckily, Georgina was gifted with one of the most important of the saving graces: a sense of humour.

Georgina continued to write, although under duress, while at the farm. At the time, Edwardian travel journals were popular, so Georgina cleverly added information and details about running a farm into her articles and papers. Her first book, *A Summer on the Canadian Prairie*, published in 1910, was followed in 1914 by *Wheat and Woman*, the story of her sojourn as a farmer in Saskatchewan. The frozen harvest in 1907 meant Georgina needed to travel to New York to flog her writing. "Oh, the hardship, the hope, the trials, the sweetness and the sadness of these two years! How I have loved the beasts, and how heartily I have hated people and things here and there, and the end of it is . . . that I have to go off with a pen to save the plough, and that by to-morrow this time I shall be on my way to New York travelling in front of the dining car minus a sleeper, certainly uncomfortable, probably hungry, and doing my level best to assure myself that—nothing matters!"

Georgina was determined to open doors for other women who wished to immigrate to Canada. Feminists of the late 20th century can thank her for much of the ground she broke, literally and culturally. "On every side my neighbours had obtained their land as a gift from the Government, or at least one hundred and sixty acres of it, and a further hundred and sixty had been added on the condition of pre-emption, which is by payment of three dollars an acre in addition to the performance of the home-stead duties; in this way a farm in every way equal to the one which cost me five thousand dollars was to be obtained by any man for nine hundred and seventy dollars."

The Honourable Frank Oliver, the minister of the interior for the Liberal government at that time, maintained that the government was justified in its refusal to expand the homestead law to allow women to claim land as easily as men could. After all, he reasoned, the land gift was designed to encourage immigrants to build homes on the prairies. Men needed wives to run the homestead, but offering land to women would only encourage their independence! Georgina's response was to soldier on: "Since there was not the smallest hope of official encouragement, the only way of going on seemed to lie in refusing to give up, so I did what I could alone and very imperfectly." In later years, Georgina trained women to farm on her wheat fields, sharing her knowledge and encouraging them to join the rebellion of independence that Minister of the Interior Oliver so feared.

Georgina was independent, but she appreciated the frequent kindnesses and assistance from her neighbours and especially the strength of her relationship with Lal and Hilaria. Lal invariably brought her a cup of tea each morning, "no matter how firmly we had decided to differ the night before." He was always there when he was needed most. In 1908, when a prairie fire raced towards her farm, the much-mocked Lal was present to face it with her. A fire would have ruined her. The sudden realization gave her strength as they watched the raging fire approach.

"I went back to my brother. 'The fire is just on us,' I said."

It was a crucial moment. They knew they had only 20 minutes to burn off the overgrown fireguard that surrounded the buildings and animals. "The wind was towards us, the stable-yard still covered with litter of threshing straw . . . we started in at our task, I working east, my brother working west. For a short space there was silence save for the muffled roar of the oncoming enemy and the banging of the damp bags with which we quenched our several fires as the flames reached the limit we ruled . . . So I set my teeth and made fresh flames, and beat them out until my hands and throat and eyes were as red-hot cinders caught in a whirlwind." Burning the old fireguard saved the farm. Georgina was helped in the last moments by her neighbours, who braved the flames once their own land was secure.

"Surely the true definition of courage is to do the thing you are afraid to do," Georgina once said when complimented on her bravery in living her life of solitude. "I know about fear, and it isn't on the prairies; on the contrary solitude here seems always healing and soothing to the mind." Georgina, in every way, was a woman who could not bear to be suffocated, not by criticism, work, hardship or ridicule. Suffocation appeared to be the one thing she feared, and perhaps this is why striking a bold new life under an open sky was her adventure of choice. When her older brother Arthur visited in 1907, they argued over the division of work. She refused to wash his towels. He resented washing his own. He told her she was living "a convict's life." Finally, the workers she had hired left for the season and so did Arthur, to her great relief. "And there came to me with the silence and the softly falling rain of that restful afternoon a deep and abiding love of solitude which, like the consoling breath of the soil, cleanses the channels of one's understanding to sun-clear vision, discovering all the arrogance and unkindness in criticism, revealing the illusion of difficulty, proving one's anger and wrath and righteous indignation and clamour for justice occasionally funny and always unworthwhile."

Georgina was described frequently as a spinster, but not much is known of her private life. A photograph taken in England before her arrival in Canada shows an attractive young woman with a somewhat defiant gaze in a typical Edwardian pose—upswept hair, long gown and a sombre demeanour. Decades later, her Canadian neighbours described her as wearing britches, leggings and big floppy hats at all times. She kept numerous cats and horses and drove a buggy despite having a car at her disposal. Georgina had intended to stay in Canada only two years. She returned to England sometime in the 1930s, after over two decades on the prairies. Hilaria, the one who hated the prairies the most, stayed behind to farm and remained in Canada until her death in 1955. She and Arthur, who had returned to farm, are buried near Fort Qu'Appelle. Georgina died in England in 1947. Her ashes are spread over the land that she described so poetically in *Wheat and Woman*.

There is no template for Georgina Binnie-Clark, no way to describe or cubbyhole or diminish her. For a woman of her background to have adamantly undertaken the purchase and maintenance of land in Canada in 1905 was a huge leap away from the safe life of the English gentlewoman. Yet it did not seem so extraordinary to her. At times she despaired: "Clothesless, bootless, penniless, wretched!" But she always rallied. She had determined to make good in Canada, and she did. "On Sunday, July 28, the sun shone in amazing brilliancy. I walked through the pasture into the twenty-five acres beyond to find the wheat in full head and in its most delicate and exquisite stage of flower. It was absolute in its beauty, so alive, so strong, so glorious—just a living, breathing blessing; and in that gleaming, silent day of rest, as I stood in the heart of the field with the lovely thing around me I was glad to think that because I came to Canada that specially clean and beautiful field of wheat was there."

5

Isabel Gunn
(1780–1861)

"Dec. 29th, 1807. An extraordinary affair occurred this morning. One of Mr. Heney's Orkney lads . . . requested me to allow him to remain in my house for a short time . . . I had not been long [in my room] before he sent one of my people, requesting the favor of speaking with me . . . [I] was much surprised to find him extended on the hearth, uttering dreadful lamentations . . . in piteous tones [he] begged me to be kind to a poor, helpless, abandoned wretch, who was not of the sex I supposed, but an unfortunate Orkney girl, pregnant, and actually in childbirth."

—FROM THE JOURNAL OF ALEXANDER HENRY (THE YOUNGER)

IF THE MAN SHE LOVED was about to leave for yet another trip across the ocean to remote Rupert's Land, the usual lot of a young Orkney woman was to pray for his swift return and make do with the jobs available: domestic labour or farm work. But Isabel Gunn decided to book passage as well—as a man. In her new identity as John Fubbister, she was engaged in 1806 for a three-year term as a labourer with the Hudson's Bay Company. The 25-year-old woman boarded the *Prince of Wales* on June 29 and left Scotland bound for Albany Factory in the New World. According to most sources, her companion and lover was John Scarth, a labourer and steersman. Scarth, who had worked for the company before, was paid £32 per annum and Fubbister was paid £8. Over the years, alternative theories have surfaced. Did she embark on this masquerade for love, or did she simply want to escape a traditional life? Some sources even speculate that she met Scarth in the New World and lost touch with her original lover.

The Hudson's Bay Company regularly employed Orkneymen for its fur-trading endeavours in Rupert's Land, as Canada was known at that time. The men from the windswept islands off the northeastern coast of Scotland were reliable servants of the company, no doubt because working in difficult, bitterly cold conditions in a strange land was generally preferable to suffering in poverty in the northern isles. They were known for their discretion and closeness.

Near the end of August, the *Prince of Wales*, with cargo and passengers, docked in Moose Factory on James Bay, at the southern tip of Hudson Bay. John Fubbister and John Scarth were sent north to Albany, also on James Bay. Several months later, they were on the move again. Fubbister was assigned to six inland trips, mostly freighting expeditions, over the next year. The *Albany Fort Journal* reported on September 9, 1806, that a group of men, including Fubbister and Scarth, were dispatched to Henley House, a small outpost about 160 kilometres upstream from Albany, with trading goods and provisions. Almost a year after arriving in Rupert's Land, Fubbister was assigned to a brigade that was to winter at the post at Pembina, in Red River Territory, much farther west, in the area now known as Manitoba. Scarth was assigned elsewhere. Fubbister and Scarth had been separated, either by choice or chance.

At Pembina, two trading posts loomed over the Red River, facing each other. Hugh Heney served as factor at the Hudson's Bay Company fort; on the other side was the North West Company fort, headed by Alexander Henry (the Younger). It was there that Fubbister was discovered, when, after the Christmas festivities at the North West Company post, she asked to remain in the chief's house. Alexander Henry continues his journal entry, saying, "In about an hour she was safely delivered of a fine boy, and that same day she was conveyed home in my cariole [a small carriage] where she soon recovered."

It seems unbelievable that Isabel could have gone undetected among the fur traders for so long. It is likely that the clothing of the workers—heavy woollens in the winter and protective netting as a barrier against insects in the summer—would have disguised her figure. Despite her pregnancy, she apparently managed to continue with her work without comment. It seems nobody guessed her true identity. Or did they? Perhaps the close-knit group of Orkneymen knew John Fubbister's true gender and chose to protect her.

The news of the impostor spread across the territory. With every retelling, the facts and the names changed. John McKay, in charge of the Hudson's Bay Company post at Brandon House, near Pembina, wrote in his journal on March 2, 1808, that "one of Haneys men has turned out to be a Woman, and was delivered of a fine boy in Mr. Henrys House, the Child was born before they could get her Breeches of." Another unattributed journal expresses sympathy for the trials of Heney: "One of Mr. Heneys men . . . died last fall on the Journey, and another was found to be a woman debauched (so she says) by John Scarth, by whom she has a Child." As the story spread across Rupert's Land, there was less and less sympathy for this woman who dared to masquerade as a man.

Some historians now regard Isabel Gunn as the first non-Native woman in the Canadian west and her son as the first non-Native baby born in the remote land. Although many of the details of Isabel's life have been obscured, the Hudson's Bay Company's records are proof of her daring pretence and eventual unmasking.

Unfortunately, once she was discovered, everything changed. As John Fubbister, Isabel had been an acceptable, even valued, labourer. As Isabel Gunn, she was sent back to Albany with her son, where she was put to work as a washerwoman. By all accounts, she was not very good at it. The company had lost a good labourer and gained a half-hearted laundress. She worked for the Hudson's Bay Company for another year and resisted returning to the Orkney Islands. She was no longer involved with John Scarth, and it seems he had no desire to see the child. In 1809, her contract ended, and she was discharged from the Hudson's Bay Company with the damning note, "We cannot think of keeping this Woman any longer, as she is of a bad Character, and has not answered the intentions for which she was detained." On September 20, 1809, Isabel and her son were sent home on the same ship that had brought her to the land of promise, the *Prince of Wales*.

A vastly different life awaited her from the one she had lived in Rupert's Land. As a male servant of the Hudson's Bay Company, however lowly, she had earned more than she ever would as a woman in the Orkney Islands. In 1851, the Scottish census listed her as living on Hellyhole Street in Stromness working as "a stocking knitter." Later, she moved, and her occupation expanded to "stocking & mitten maker," a far cry from riding barges through the wilderness on the Red River. Some reports say Isabel and her children fell on hard times, reportedly becoming vagrants. When she died on November 7, 1861, her obituary listed her as "a pauper and single." Her passing was listed in a local paper: "At Stromness, a few days ago, Isabella Gunn [died], at an advanced age, Isabel in her youthful days, dressed herself in male attire, and went out to Hudson Bay, in search of her lover, and lived there for sometime ere her sex was discovered."

Isabel Gunn's story has been embroidered, stretched and reshaped to suit the tellers: some say she was a lumberjack, or an unfortunate, pathetic creature, others call her a witch. Various versions of her relationship with Scarth surface; her name is even spelled several different ways. Two centuries later, the elusive, rebellious Isabel remains a mystery.

6

Caroline Fulham
(1852–unknown)

"Mrs. Fulham, who was without doubt the best known woman in Calgary, passed through the city on Monday night. She informed some of those at the station that she was coming back to live here in six weeks. This news will be received with mingled feelings."

—*CALGARY HERALD*, 1905

THE EDWARDIAN VIEW OF WOMEN was only slightly advanced from that of the Victorian era. They were expected to be gentle, loving helpmates and competent, quiet chatelaines. The majority of women may have been a civilizing influence on the West, but Caroline Fulham was not one of them. In fact, the reverse may have been true. What was frontier Calgary to do with noisy Mother

Caroline Fulham, known (by all) and fondly regarded (by some) as the Pig Lady?

Not much is known about Caroline Fulham, except that she was the most notorious woman in Calgary at the turn of the 20th century. For 15 years from 1889, she lived in downtown Calgary. Her husband, variously described as a decent, inoffensive man or a rolling stone, had retreated to a ranch west of Calgary, coming into town only when summoned by Caroline. The infrequency of his visits may have been due to the incident in which she reportedly sent him down a well, then removed the ladder and left him there for the night. Her decidedly indecorous occupation was that of pig keeper. She and her infamous pigs reigned at 612 6th Avenue SW in a small cottage with a backyard. With no restricting bylaws, the neighbours could do nothing but groan and hold their noses. To feed her darlings, Caroline toured the hotel kitchens of the Royal, the Grand Central, the Alberta, the Windsor and the Queens, as well as the Criterion and New Brunswick cafés, with a large swill barrel on the back of the little cart pulled by her horse Billy.

Caroline, with her loud voice, Irish accent, outrageous vocabulary and uncombed hair, created a commotion wherever she went. She was quick-tempered, quick-witted and strong enough to lift a barrel of swill into her wagon single-handedly, and people learned the hard way not to get between her and her garbage. As she drove down Stephen Avenue with the reins in her dirty hands, a clay pipe in her mouth and her temper rarely in check, most people wisely tried to keep out of her way.

Not surprisingly, Mother Fulham was not known for her cleanliness. An infamous incident relating to her lamentable lack of personal hygiene involved Dr. Harry Goodsir McKidd, who had offered to look at her sore ankle. When she rolled down her stocking, he was stunned by the sight of her filthy leg. "I'll bet you five dollars, Mrs. Fulham, there isn't a dirtier leg in all of Calgary," gasped the doctor. Caroline gleefully shouted, "I'll take that bet, Doctor," and rolled down her other stocking to reveal an equally filthy leg. The good doctor paid up.

Caroline was reportedly the only woman to go drinking with all-male clientele at the Alberta Hotel, a fine sandstone building on the southeast corner of 1st Street West and Stephen Avenue. The north side of the avenue was where the ladies walked; the south side was where Caroline was comfortable. She reportedly matched the men at the hotel bar drink for drink—and more. She constantly ended up in hot water with the local police, most frequently for public misdemeanours related to her short fuse or her alcohol level, a lethal combination in the system of a feisty, plump and thoroughly uninhibited Irishwoman. It generally took at least three policemen to subdue this gentle flower of Edwardian womanhood when she was in full sail. The courtroom was always packed whenever she and lawyer Paddy Nolan teamed up to foil the law, evade punishment or create a forum for her peculiar sense of justice. She had formed a mutually satisfying alliance with Nolan, a fellow Irish immigrant, and the two of them raised (or lowered) courtroom appearances to the level of comic opera mixed with vaudeville. Apparently she never paid Nolan, who liked the full courtrooms. Everybody showed up, so it was great promotion for Nolan. For Caroline, it was a chance to shout back at the world.

Nice Edwardian ladies did not shout. They did not even raise their voices. But Caroline was not a typical lady of her time. When her cow wandered onto the Canadian Pacific Railway (CPR) tracks and was killed by an inconsiderate train, she sued the CPR. When the "No Trespassing" sign was noted by the opposing lawyers, she shouted, "You damn fools! Do you think me cow could read?" Not satisfied with the judgment, she continued to complain, even after a private meeting with CPR president Sir William Van Horne in his railway car.

Caroline was never one to flee from a fight. In fact, she loved to start them. If it looked as if a conflict might begin to cool, she masterfully stoked the fires. She appeared at the offices of the *Calgary Herald* on October 21, 1901. "Good morning to you young man, an' it's an ill-used woman I am this day." She placed a pile of dark grey hair on the desk and removed her hat, saying, "The bastes of policemen tore that from me head." The torn hair was later revealed to match the mane and tail of her horse. True to form, she had spent the night in jail, put up a good fight and then decided to demand recompense for her suffering.

Mother Fulham was sometimes repaid for her combative ways with practical jokes. Once, her pony was rehitched to her buggy while she was enjoying a long session at the bar in the Alberta Hotel. The horse ended up on the opposite side of the fence from the buggy. Caroline emerged from the hotel, inebriated, tried to drive, then figured it out and went searching for the delinquents with her buggy whip. Another night, on Saint Patrick's Day, her pigs were painted emerald green while she was celebrating in the style that only she could achieve.

But Caroline could give as good as she got. She may not have been a fashionable woman, but she certainly had her own style. On July 12, 1889, the day of the parade of the Orange Lodge, the historic Protestant fraternal organization, Caroline dressed up, but not in orange. She had gone to the Hudson's Bay Company store and bought a wide silk ribbon in bright green. She draped it from her neck to her knees, topped it with a huge green bow and, so adorned, shamelessly heckled the Orangemen in the passing parade.

Yet she had her allies. Some pals escorted Caroline to the annual Fireman's Ball, the social event of the season, held at the Hull Opera House, at Centre Street and 6th Avenue. She wore a long evening ensemble of brilliant paddy green and leaned over the balcony overlooking the dancers, providing her dates with raucous gossip.

There are many anecdotes about Mother Fulham, but only a few remembrances that reveal a more well-rounded character. Although the much-repeated stories of her riotous behaviour are entertaining, less well known are the references to her rough-edged generosity. She was known to spontaneously lend money to those in need. A farmer whose horses had died was treated to the vision of a rolled-down stocking, a dirty ankle, a roll of money and $40 pressed into his hand for a new horse. Perhaps she was a woman who decided at some early age not to take any guff from anybody, and she certainly didn't.

Caroline Fulham was not a gentlewoman; she was an in-your-face vulgarian. Cleanliness was not a priority. Silence was a horror. Deference was unknown and delicacy a hilarious concept. For better or worse, she rebelled against what society expected of her. Scorned, laughed at, ridiculed and enjoyed as a source of entertainment, her scandalous behaviour probably allowed or encouraged one, or two, or twenty women to behave in ways that defied the norm. She pushed the boundaries for what women could be in frontier Calgary.

She left Calgary in 1904, after her husband's death. ("I cried with both eyes," she told a friend.) The police department was delighted to see the last of her, but the townspeople of Calgary had lost their free entertainment. Amazingly, the Pig Lady reportedly left Calgary with $33,000 in cash, an impressive sum in those days, thanks to shrewd real-estate investments. She settled in Vancouver, where she ran a restaurant. (One wonders about the wisdom of eating there, given her history in hygiene.) She married again, briefly, to a Vancouver confidence artist—a marriage that lasted a year. In 1905, she passed through Calgary, then disappeared.

7

Georgia Engelhard
(1902–1986)

"The lake and valley were still in deep shadow, but the surrounding peaks, all I had climbed, were bathed in golden rosy light. I was seized by an indescribable ecstasy, filled with the joy of conquest. They were all mine—my beautiful, private world of mountains. Yet, at the same time, I felt how infinitesimal I was. It was an unforgettable experience."

—GEORGIA ENGELHARD IN *LAKE LOUISE DAYS*

YOUNG GEORGIA WAS AFRAID OF HEIGHTS. For most young women of her era, this would not have presented a problem. In the early 1900s, women of her class would have very few encounters with anything higher than the several floors of stairs in the family home. But Georgia came from a culturally aware New York family, which gave her the means to travel and the thirst for experience. So instead of hiding on the main floor of life, she learned to climb mountains.

Georgia Engelhard (later Georgia Engelhard Cromwell) was a multi-talented artist who became one of North America's leading mountaineers, with over 32 first ascents and innumerable other climbs in the Canadian Rockies and European Alps to her credit.

She grew up in an atmosphere of creativity and achievement. Her father was a lawyer and amateur musician. Her mother's brother was famed photographer Alfred Stieglitz, who was married to the artist Georgia O'Keeffe. She spent summers at the Stieglitz family estate at Lake George, New York, where she learned to play poker, showed talent as an artist with early drawings and watercolours and exercised her irrepressible wit. At the age of 13, Georgia so impressed the formidable O'Keeffe that the two spent much time together. Engelhard was nicknamed "Georgia Minor."

Georgia enrolled at Vassar in 1923, but she grew restless. "I'm surging with the desire to face actuality—to do something by myself. Maybe I'm foolish—maybe I'll be disappointed or disillusioned—but rather that than this horrible passivity, this demoralizing stagnation." She transferred to Columbia University to study art. Art classes stimulated her, but she yearned for her own home and independence from her family. Her style of painting began to resemble O'Keeffe's. Perhaps this is why she transferred again, this time to the New York Institute of Photography. She began to freelance and sold photographs to magazines, a signpost to one of the careers she would successfully pursue several decades later.

Not content to be a talented watercolourist and promising photographer, Georgia also took horse-riding lessons and participated several times at the International Horse Show in Madison Square Gardens. It seemed as if her talents were so abundant that she needed to find one that was exclusively hers, outside the realm of her loving but excessively accomplished family.

She had visited the Alps with her family and found mountain climbing "a perfectly idiotic sport." A family holiday at Mount Rainier National Park in Washington in 1926 changed that opinion. Her father persuaded her to try rock climbing. She and a guide made the 2,000-metre climb up Pinnacle Peak, usually a one-day climb, in half a day. They stopped next at Lake Louise in the Canadian Rockies, where she climbed another Pinnacle Peak (3,067 metres) and then Mount Temple and Mount Whyte. After that, there was no stopping her. "In those early days there were no climbing schools for the novice. You learned while climbing—watching the Guide's motions and taking in the few instructions he gave you," wrote Georgia in *Lake Louise Days*.

Georgia came back to the Rockies in 1927 and continued to add mountain after mountain to her list of conquests. In 1929, she climbed nine peaks in nine days, including Lefroy,

Haddo, Aberdeen, Hungabee, Huber, Victoria and Biddle. She was known as a fast climber. Somehow, the young woman who had been afraid of heights as a child was racing up mountains with enthusiastic élan. One guide, Ernest Feuz, warned another, "You've got a fine lady, but watch out. When she starts uphill, she goes like a rocket. What she needs is a mountain goat, not a guide!"

In a letter written years later, Georgia said, "I was twenty years old, slim, with enormously strong legs and great endurance. Our climbs were always made in pretty fast time and quite without incidents or hair-raising experiences. With my slight frame, close-cropped hair and fly front pants, I was often ejected from Ladies Rooms or Beer Parlors where I was taken for a teen age boy. Even in latter years, when I was in my mid-thirties people would accost me and say, 'Sonny, your daddy taking you hiking?'"

In 1931, Georgia made 38 ascents in Yoho National Park and the Selkirk Mountains, including Chancellor Peak (3,280 metres), an ascent she described in the 1932 *Canadian Alpine Journal*. She and her guide, Ernest Feuz, drove from Wapta Falls Camp in the Yoho Valley to the forest at the base of the peak. The climb was 274 metres. "We kept ourselves from slipping, which would have been fatal, mainly by friction holds with our feet and knees, our fingers clinging desperately to a slight knot or crack that presented itself on the smooth rock face." They reached the summit of Chancellor after eight and a half hours of continuous

In 1931, Georgia Engelhard and guide Ernest Feuz climbed Mount Victoria in Banff National Park. GLENBOW ARCHIVES NA-4868-197

climbing. At the summit, the discovery of a note deeply moved her. The Sir James Outram party, the first group to gain the peak in 1901, had left it. "It was indeed an awesome moment," she wrote, "and I felt a great thrill at the thought of ours being the second party to stand on that lofty summit, almost exactly thirty years after it was first conquered."

Georgia also climbed the steepled peak of Mount Victoria (3,464 metres), near the Alberta–British Columbia border in Banff National Park, several times in 1931. One trip was for the filming of the movie *She Climbs to Conquer*, filmed by Canadian Pacific Railway cameraman Bill Oliver. During the filming, she and the crew were caught on South Peak in a horrific thunderstorm. "The thunder was deadening and boomed back and forth from the rock walls, the lightning struck the rocks causing them to sing and spit flame. Our nailed boots and ice axes also spit fire, our hair stood on end." She experienced all this before she was even 26 years old. Georgia had come a long way from the placid summers at Lake George.

Georgia, with her Uncle Alfred's encouragement, became a competent photographer and, with O'Keeffe's coaching, an interesting painter. Her work has been described as "a simplification of shapes; shining, luminous surfaces; and a certain radiance about her colors, a muted internal brilliance, particularly in her whites."

In 1935, Georgia travelled to Europe and climbed in the Alps with Eaton "Tony" Cromwell, the man who eventually became her husband. They were climbing partners and companions for a number of years before he divorced his estranged wife. Georgia and Tony were well matched: both were excellent climbers, energetic, competitive and (a great boon for a climber) both financially independent.

Georgia continued to climb in the Rockies, reporting many of her hair-raising experiences in *The Canadian Alpine Journal*. In 1936, in her article "New Routes in the Rockies," she described the descent from a traverse of Glacier Peak. "It was extremely steep and we were carefully making our way down it, when a huge boulder came bounding toward us from the Ringrose side. The slope was too steep to allow us to move out of our steps, but fortunately we were spared by the margin of a foot."

In 1939, Georgia embarked on the "Bobbie Burns Adventure." She was determined to climb the peaks of the Bobbie Burns group in the Bugaboo Mountains, 300 kilo-metres west of Calgary, a feat that had never been attempted before. Accompanied by a guide, a companion and a num-ber of pack horses, she started from their camp at the foot of the Bugaboo moraine. The group followed an old min-ing trail upward. By noon, they had reached a deserted mining cabin at 1,200 metres set amid "fine big alplands with clusters of larch trees." They continued climbing to 2,400 metres, then followed a tortuous route of numerous climbs and descents to reach the Bobbie Burns slopes. The triumphant group descended, moving at the agonizingly slow rate of less than one kilometre every two hours, working their way over rocks and fallen timber. The horses were exhausted, and the packs kept slipping. When the group finally battled down to what they hoped were meadows, they found a bug-infested swamp. In Georgia's words: "Sand in the water, sand in the food, in the beds, in the duffle, in the clothes, plus a fine assortment of very vicious bull-dog flies, mosquitoes and sand-gnats. But here we were, the very first people ever to camp on Bobbie Burns creek at the base of its towering peaks—lords of a valley heretofore unvisited except perhaps by an occasional trapper. All of which was very satisfying to contemplate."

Georgia may have conquered the mountains, but she also appears to have intimidated the guides, drawing both admiration and raised eyebrows from the usually reticent mountain experts. It was said that she was viewed as "difficult," in part because she always carried her own load and had more endurance and strength than some of the men. It doesn't seem to have bothered her. Her focus was on the mountains, not on what people thought of her.

Georgia and Cromwell were married in 1947. They settled in the Swiss Alps and lived there until their deaths in the mid-1980s. Surprisingly, after her huge successes in the Canadian Rockies, Georgia had no desire to return, saying she feared her illusions would be shattered by the inevitable changes to the wilderness she had loved and conquered.

The exuberant Georgia had climbed the majestic peaks

of the Rockies in defiance of her childhood fears. She wanted to be independent. To climb a mountain, and to be the first, was something that was hers. She wrote, "Why do I like climbing? Why do you like bridge? I don't know. It's a disease and chronic, I fear. Perhaps it's the excitement, perhaps it's the beauty of the escape from conventional comforts."

Today, Engelhard Tower, at the head of Bison Creek in Banff National Park, a peak first ascended in 1938 by Georgia, is a lasting tribute to the young rebel who dashed up mountains.

CHAPTER

8

Tookoolito
(1838–1876)

"Simple and gentle in her way, there was a degree of calm intellectual power abut her that more and more astonished me."

—CHARLES FRANCIS HALL

HOW DID A QUIET INUIT WOMAN from Cumberland Sound take tea with Queen Victoria, then, years later, survive a nightmarish six months on a drifting ice floe in the Arctic?

Tookoolito, also known as Hannah, Taqulittuq or Tackritow, was an extraordinary woman. Born on Baffin Island in the Canadian Arctic in 1838, she worked with a number of Arctic explorers and adventurers as a teacher and interpreter of the Inuit language and culture. Eventually, she became fluent in English, an unusual feat for an Inuit woman of those times. She and her husband, Ebierbing, an Inuit hunter also known as Joe, or Ipirvik, sailed to England in 1853 with whaling captain Thomas Bowlby and were presented to Queen Victoria. Eventually, they lived in Connecticut when not travelling the Far North in rigorous conditions.

Just as there are variations in Tookoolito's name, due to the translation from the Inuit language, so, after nearly two centuries, there are varying reports on her meeting with the British monarch. Whether it was tea at Buckingham Palace or dinner at Windsor Castle, the meeting left a strong impression on both parties. Tookoolito and Ebierbing spent 20 months in England, along with an unrelated Inuit child; alas, there seem to be no chronicles of what this poor displaced child thought of the experience.

Tookoolito, while in England, made a quantum leap in adaptation. How many women, displaced from a remote culture based on hunting and living off the land, would be able to adapt to a world in which tea was taken, stockings were knitted and raw seal meat was not on the daily menu? Tookoolito did that and more. She was far from her birthplace in Cumberland Sound and the vicious weather of the North. Although she and Ebierbing had been married in the Inuit tradition for some years, the relationship was formalized in England in a wedding at the home of John Bowlby.

Tookoolito wore silk finery and adopted the niceties of English living. By the time she and her husband returned to the Arctic, she was a strange mix of British upper-class cultivation and Inuit survival know-how. She learned English to the extent that her voice was said to be not much different from the cultivated voices one would hear in British society. "That tone instantly told me that a lady of refinement was there, greeting me," wrote Charles Francis Hall in his diary. He had been surprised to hear a female voice on the whaling boat *George Henry*. He looked up from his desk and was astonished. "Could I be dreaming? Was it a mistake? No! I was wide awake and writing."

What had so shocked him was the image of a small woman in a flounced dress, caribou jacket and Victorian bonnet. He was even more surprised when the light fell on her face and he discovered she was the Inuit woman called Hannah, or Tookoolito, who was much respected by the whalers. He had hoped to meet her and secure her services as an interpreter, but had not expected a person so adept at European dress and speech. Tookoolito spoke fluent English, more so than her husband, who was described by Hall as "a fine, and also intelligent-looking man."

Tookoolito said of Queen Victoria, "I visited her, and liked the appearance of her majesty, and every thing about the palace. Fine place, I assure you, sir." Queen Victoria, in turn, had described Tookoolito and Joe in her diary, writing, "They are my subjects, very curious & quite different to any of the southern or African tribes, having very flat round faces, with a Mongolian shape of eyes, a fair skin, & jet black hair."

As for Hall, his admiration was immediate and constant.

"I could not help admiring the exceeding gracefulness and modesty of her demeanour. Simple and gentle in her way, there was a degree of calm intellectual power about her that more and more astonished me."

On returning to the place of their birth, Tookoolito and Ebierbing were much in demand. They spoke English, had some understanding of British culture and were an experienced team of interpreter and guide.

Hall, a relatively inexperienced explorer, was in search of the lost Franklin expedition and then the North Pole. He still needed to raise money for the latter expedition, but in the meantime, he was eager to travel north. He immediately recognized the potential usefulness of this extraordinary couple. He wrote, "I feel greater confidence . . . in the success of my mission since engaging these two natives. They can talk with me in my own vernacular, are both smart, and will be useful each in the department they will be called upon to fill."

Tookoolito and Ebierbing joined Hall on two Arctic expeditions, 1860–62 and 1864–69. While the American Civil War raged in the South, Hall and his companions endured sub-zero temperatures and lethal, frigid seas in the North. The couple also helped Hall with fundraising for the expeditions, appearing with him at podiums, along with their infant son.

The unfortunate Hall had no idea that, a few years later, these two would be testifying about his murder by arsenic poisoning, administered by an unknown member of his crew on the doomed 1871 Polaris expedition. Tookoolito was one of two Inuit women on this voyage to the North Pole led by Hall. By then, she and Ebierbing had known Hall for some years, and the explorer had come to regard the couple as mentors. They were loyal to him, and the trio had developed a friendship of sorts.

After Hall's sudden death, the situation aboard the *Polaris* became chaotic. There was infighting among the crew and a lack of true leadership. Then the ship was damaged by the ice through which she travelled and became trapped. On the evening of October 15, 1872, Tookoolito and 18 others from the expedition were separated from the *Polaris* and abandoned on a large ice floe in a freak accident. While the crewmen were in the process of throwing supplies onto the ice floe in anticipation of abandoning ship, the damaged ship broke free of the ice and drifted away, with the 19 on the floe signalling desperately for its return. They drifted inexorably southward for 1,500 miles and 190 days, in sub-zero temperatures, surviving on raw seal meat caught by the Inuit hunters in the group. It was the Inuit, including Tookoolito, who were reportedly responsible for the survival of the group, headed by the ranking officer George E. Tyson.

Many accounts of the ordeal overlook the contribution of the Inuit. Yet Tyson's diary records that without the Inuit presence they would have perished. Tookoolito, Ebierbing and a Greenlandic Inuit hunter, Hans Hendrik, kept the stranded group alive with their survival skills. The remnants of the ship's crew would not have known how to build igloos or hunt for seal. They lived in a small group of igloos, linked by passages, on the drifting—and shrinking— ice floe. The desperate group drifted past Greenland and Baffin Island until they were finally rescued off the coast of Newfoundland by a sealing boat, *Tigress*, on April 30, 1873.

Tookoolito and Ebierbing returned to their two-storey house in Groton, Connecticut, where she worked as a seamstress, while Ebierbing on occasion returned to the Arctic to work as a guide. Tookoolito had been heartbroken by the death of two infant sons years earlier. She and her husband had adopted an Inuit girl named Panik, who had been on the floe with them. Panik died at the age of nine from pneumonia, her system weakened by the ordeal in the Arctic. Tookoolito became despondent, and her health declined. She died of tuberculosis in December 1876.

Despite her short life, Tookoolito made a significant contribution to Arctic exploration and earned respect for herself and the Inuit people. Her name lives on, not only in history, but also in the Arctic. Tookoolito Inlet in Nunavut is a permanent record of the courage and endurance of a woman who lived in both the formal world of Victorian England and the brutal Far North.

9

Katherine Stinson
(1891–1977)

CALGARY EXHIBITION 1916: Over the upturned heads of 40,000 spectators, a biplane swooped through daring aerial manoeuvres, including one of the most dangerous stunts ever performed: a loop-the-loop. The plane landed safely, and the crowd roared its approval. The cockpit door opened and the daredevil pilot emerged, pulling off a flying helmet. Long curls, adorable dimples and a stunning smile completed the performance. This was Katherine Stinson, dubbed The Flying Schoolgirl.

KATHERINE STINSON WAS BORN FEBRUARY 14, 1891, in Alabama. She had planned to study piano in Europe and eventually teach music, an interesting but not unusual choice of career for a young woman of her time. But where would she find $1,000 to finance her studies? The concept of flying intrigued her, and she had heard that barnstorming stunt pilots were making $1,000 a day for risking their lives for the crowds. Before commercial aviation, fliers earned big bucks flying at fairgrounds and agricultural exhibitions. To her parents' amazement, she sold her piano so that she could take flying lessons.

These were the early days of aviation. Women simply did not fly airplanes. They were barely capable of mastering the mechanics of a car, according to popular wisdom. The first pilot who took Katherine up in a plane tried his best to discourage her by subjecting her to what he assumed would be a terrifying ordeal. He failed miserably. She wasn't frightened at all. "Instead of being cured of my ambition, as I think Mr. Jannus hoped, I came down more eager than ever to become a flyer myself." Not intimidated, but unable to find someone who would teach her to fly, Katherine went to Chicago to meet Maximillian Liljestrand, known in flying circles as Max Lillie. He agreed to enrol her in his flying school in May 1912.

Although she was petite, Katherine had a natural dexterity and excellent reflexes. She earned her pilot's licence on July 24, 1912, at the age of 21, only the fourth female pilot in the United States to do so. Somewhere along the way, her birthdate mysteriously changed, and she became 16 again, billing herself as The Flying Schoolgirl. One look at the adorable imp who emerged from the cockpit after a stunt and who could doubt her youthful exuberance? Her manager, Bill Pickens, recalled, "There she was, a wisp of a thing with big brown eyes, an engaging soft southern drawl and pink ribbons in her long curls. She didn't look a day over sixteen." Katherine wisely kept her true age to herself and let people guess.

Flying at that time was not comfortable. The pilot perched on narrow rigging and was subjected to ferocious winds and cold temperatures. He or she had to lean to one side to turn the plane, with no seat belt. Many fell to their death.

From 1916 to 1918, Katherine barnstormed across western Canada, wowing crowds in Edmonton, Brandon, Regina, Winnipeg and Calgary with double loops and daring dives. The latter so alarmed a crowd in Regina that the local newspaper received many calls from people convinced she had crashed. But the young woman who knew her planes' mechanics inside out, who rebuilt engines and obsessively checked maintenance, never had a serious mishap. In 1916, after one of her afternoon shows at the Calgary Exhibition, she leaped back in her plane and flew to a military camp, Camp Sarcee, for dinner with the officers, many of whom were fascinated by her aircraft and, no doubt, charmed by the lady herself. She then flew back to the exhibition grounds for the evening show.

A few days after her fete at Camp Sarcee, she decided, on a rebellious whim, to visit another army camp, this time in Manitoba. When she made a surprise landing at Camp Hughes, soldiers with bayonets thought she was a German spy and briefly carted her off to prison. One can only imagine the looks on the faces of the military personnel when a crackerjack pilot made an expert landing on their parade grounds and climbed out of the cockpit looking like the most unlikely person imaginable: diminutive, dimpled and "as pretty as an angel."

In 1917, after three of her Calgary shows were cancelled due to unexpected repairs, the *Morning Albertan* wrote: "After a wearisome effort Miss Katherine Stinson, who has been having bad luck with her flying machines, succeeded in setting up her smaller, one passenger biplane and promptly at four o'clock, she made a beautiful flight over the grand stand, circling and looping gracefully in the sky and making a perfect landing in front of the grand stand. Last night she made a spectacular flight at nine o'clock with the plane electrically luminated, and the vision of the machine whirling high [in] the air, spangled with lights, was a vision which few who were present will forget." Despite the praise, Katherine flew into Calgary unexpectedly for the 1918 exhibition, reportedly because she wanted to compensate for the cancelled performances of the preceding year. She moved on to Edmonton, Lethbridge and Red Deer within the next week, performing for the eager crowds.

The eagerness of her Canadian fans was almost fatal. Outside of Toronto, Montreal and Vancouver, few people had seen an actual aircraft. A crowd had gathered around her plane, inspecting the huge piece of newfangled machinery.

"Just before I started, a woman came up to the machine and said that she had dropped her glove in there. I looked for it and felt around under the seat but couldn't find it." But when she got into the air, she couldn't turn. The pulley was jammed and only a left-hand turn was possible. "It made me pretty uncomfortable. I kept fussing away, hoping to get the pulley free, it simply wouldn't work. By manoeuvring around, I managed to land safely. And when I investigated, there was the missing glove, caught in the mechanism of the controls."

In 1916, Katherine agreed to fly in Winnipeg to raise money for the Patriotic Fund. The sky was overcast and believed to be too dark for her performance. People waited, excited about the performance but anxious about the danger. She chose not to delay the flight any further and took off into the almost black sky. Those who drove motorcars were asked to park them around the perimeter of the fairground with their headlights on. Soldiers stood by with flare guns, and bonfires were started to light her descent. She rose to 304 metres and ignited flares on the rear wings, so that the crowd below could see her plane flying and dancing through the dark clouds. When she landed, the crowd was "delirious" with excitement.

Although she was an American, Katherine Stinson earned her place in western Canadian history in 1918, by flying the first airmail flight between Calgary and Edmonton. Plagued by mechanical difficulties and uncooperative weather, she triumphed over circumstances and

Aviatrix Katherine Stinson in Calgary in 1917, where she astonished onlookers with a daring evening performance. GLENBOW ARCHIVES NA-3965-64

flew her Curtiss Stinson Special biplane from Calgary to Edmonton. In Calgary, postmaster G.C. King handed her a bag that contained 259 letters, each of which was stamped "Aeroplane Mail Service, July 9, 1918, Calgary, Alberta" in violet ink. Eleven kilometres north of Calgary, a loose bolt in the carburetor forced her to land. Mechanics were summoned, and she flew back to Calgary to begin the flight again. In Edmonton, crowds gathered to watch her taxi up the runway and hand the bag to the Edmonton postmaster George Armstrong, while the ever-present photographers captured the beaming smile that always accompanied her achievements. The flight was the second airmail flight in Canada, and Katherine had set a record, flying 281 kilometres in two hours and five minutes. On July 20, 1918, *The Farm and Ranch Review* reported that "the trip was accomplished by the girl aviator, Katherine Stinson, who not only by her pluck and perseverance but by her general charm and friendliness has endeared herself to the Western Canadian people."

Katherine and her family opened the Stinson School of Flying in San Antonio in 1916, purchasing the land for an airfield with the money from Katherine's lucrative stunt work in the skies. Katherine Stinson, The Flying Schoolgirl and now flight instructor, was accomplished enough to teach men how to fly, yet her application to enlist as a pilot for the First World War was rejected because of her gender. Instead, she flew across the United States, dropping Red Cross

Katherine Stinson receiving mail from the Calgary postmaster for the first air mail flight in western Canada. GLENBOW ARCHIVES NA-520-1

pamphlets over cities as part of the war effort, and in the process creating tremendous press for the Red Cross. "She flew at night and landed on race tracks, threading her way through trees, buildings and telegraph wires by the light of an old-fashioned bonfire of barrels and hay, and never had a serious accident," recalled Bill Pickens.

Single minded about her abilities and her choices, Katherine was determined to participate in the war in Europe. In 1918, she became a driver for Mrs. Harriman's Ambulance Corps on the battlefields of France. Her

mother found out through the following telegram: "DEAR
MOTHER STOP GOING TO FRANCE STOP WILL DRIVE AMBU-
LANCE FOR THE RED CROSS STOP SEE YOU AFTER THE WAR
STOP LOVE KATHERINE END."

In her seven-year career, Katherine was the first woman to
fly solo at night, the first woman to fly over London, England,
and the first woman in the world to loop-the-loop (at Chicago
in 1915). Katherine taught herself that manoeuvre, because
the few male pilots who knew it refused to instruct a woman
in such a dangerous stunt. She invented the "dippy twist"
loop, a vertical bank in which the aircraft rolls at the top of
the loop, and was one of the first women pilots to perform
skywriting. She told reporters, "When I looped-the-loop last
July, it was a bitter pill for the male pilots to swallow, but I
accomplished all their stunts and in my case went them one
better." She did not mention that male pilots resented her
because they felt that a mere female performing the stunts
would denigrate the value of the deed. Katherine also raised
over two million dollars in pledges for the Red Cross, and set
numerous distance and endurance records.

Was she ever afraid? Her answer to that question may
explain the ease with which she decided to become a pilot.
"My mother never warned me not to do this or that for fear
of being hurt. Of course I got hurt, but I was never afraid. If
I think my machine is all right and I know I can manage it,
I am not afraid." Although Katherine appeared to live life
dangerously, she took calculated risks. "I have been flying

when a thunderstorm would come and the lightning would streak right between the wings of my machine. It is a very curious thing to see it so close to you. I wasn't in the least frightened at the time. But, later, when I heard of an airplane being struck by lightning when it was up in a thunderstorm, I decided not to take any more chances of that kind."

Katherine Stinson was an unusual young woman who created her own place despite her girlish appearance and birth into a society that limited women's opportunities. She broke through the barriers of sexism. She fixed her eyes on the stars and knew that she could fly among them. She proved it to an entranced public again and again and became a celebrity in her time.

Katherine contracted tuberculosis while serving in France, which ended her flying career. She moved to Santa Fe, New Mexico, to recover her health. At the Sunmount Sanitarium, she became interested in the architecture of the area, which was based on a blend of centuries-old Spanish and Pueblo Indian culture. After her discharge, she earned her contractor's licence and began buying and remodelling adobe homes. She married a fellow pilot, lawyer Miguel A. Otero, Jr. He became a judge. Never one to retire from achievement or bold endeavour, Katherine became a renowned architect, continuing to forge new paths in what had been a man's world.

10

Mary Percy Jackson (1904–2000)

"I had never met a woman doctor. I just wanted to be one, so that was that."

—MARY PERCY JACKSON

IN 1929, MARY PERCY ARRIVED in the Peace River country in northern Alberta to practise medicine. As the sole doctor covering a 560–square kilometre area of isolated home-steaders, she reached her patients on horseback. At 25 years of age, she had just graduated from medical school in England. She considered herself fortunate that some of the male professors had tested the resilience of the women students by giving them the toughest tasks; it prepared her for life in Battle River Prairie, Alberta.

The advertisement in the *British Medical Journal* in

February 1929 read: "Strong energetic medical women with post-graduate experience in midwifery, wanted for country work in western Canada." When Mary discovered that the ability to ride a horse was listed as a distinct advantage, she rejoiced: "Marvelous! Doctoring on horseback in a remote area of a northern forest!"

Mary had known she wanted to be a physician from the time she was 11. She excelled as a medical student in London, winning the Queen's Prize for best all-round student. As a house physician and surgeon at various hospitals, she gained valuable experience and was considered to have a bright future ahead of her as a successful doctor in England.

By the time she graduated in 1927, women were starting to move into jobs previously held only by men. It was the era of the "New Woman." In northern Alberta, other changes had occurred: the fur-trading wilderness had become homesteading land. With the arrival of women and families came a need for appropriate medical care, particularly for childbirth. In the 1920s, the maternal mortality rate in rural Canada was three times that of Britain. The United Farm Women of Alberta exerted pressure on the Alberta government to provide competent medical care for women and children in remote areas like the Peace River country.

As medicine was still a relatively new field for women, the safest choice for Mary would have been a practice close to home. But instead of a conventional practice in England,

Mary considered Calcutta as a destination. Then she saw the fateful advertisement that changed her life.

At the time, the Canadian government was recruiting female doctors for the North. Women could be paid less, and the life was so gruelling that few men would choose it, given the other options available to them. The government propaganda glossed over the hardships and emphasized the adventure. Mary sailed to Canada with two other women, each blissfully unaware of what really lay ahead.

Mary arrived in Edmonton in June 1929 and became part of a travelling clinic of two dentists, two doctors and four nurses. They had six tents that were used as an operating theatre, a hospital and housing. She loved it, but waited impatiently for a permanent posting and a place she could call home. Then the nurse in Battle River Prairie broke her arm, and Mary was sent to replace her.

The trip north, with the superintendent district nurse accompanying her, took 24 hours by train to Peace River. It was a further 18 hours by boat down the Peace River, laden with 22 boxes and 453 kilograms of supplies, and then another 28 kilometres by wagon to Battle River Prairie. The trip was complicated by the fact that the women, wearing dresses, coats and hats, had to haul all the boxes up a steep bank that the wagon couldn't negotiate when full. They persevered through thick swarms of mosquitoes, stopping en route to make tea from a mud hole. Those last 28 kilometres took 11 gruelling hours to complete. Mary walked most of the last part of the journey in temperatures that reached 35°C in the shade. "I must say I liked the idea of going into a new country with all my goods on a wagon and me walking behind in true homesteader style, but there are more comfortable ways of travelling."

Finally, she reached her new home, a little wooden shack by the Notikewin River. The nearest hospital was 160 kilometres away in Peace River. There was no electric power, no phones, and there were three rivers she would have to cross in order to reach her patients. The house was filthy, due to the muddy boots that had trekked through it in the excitement of her predecessor's accident. Years later, she noted: "I came out with luxuries, but not the necessities." The key to Mary Percy's success was that she found the situation funny and exhilarating. "People these days would call it a challenge. I thought it was hilarious!" she wrote to her family in one of her many letters home that documented her years in the bush. In her shack, which was just over four metres by six metres, she examined patients, maintained a dispensary and kept her living quarters.

Mary's first patient was a Native man, Mr. Bottle, who hadn't slept for three nights because of toothache. He arrived on her doorstep and demanded she pull his tooth, warning her that his teeth were extremely difficult to extract. "Well, I looked at it, an upper wisdom tooth, half way down his throat nearly! However there's not a dentist nearer than Peace River, 100 miles away, so I went for it. Bared my right

Dr. Mary Percy at the district doctor's cottage, Battle River Prairie (also called Notikewin), Alberta. GLENBOW ARCHIVES NA-3953-9

brawny arm and gave a colossal pull—and nearly went backwards through the window. It came out as easily as any other tooth!! I was awfully bucked, of course, and he could hardly believe his eyes. My reputation as a dentist will certainly spread!"

Despite the exuberance in her letters, there were a few early moments when she nearly gave up. "I was strongly tempted, except there was no possible way of getting out of the place once I got there . . . By the end of a month's time when I could have got out of there, wild horses wouldn't have dragged me away. This was really quite thrilling." In Canada, Mary had the freedom to be an independent woman. At times, she wondered about life back in England, then confessed that the thought of a street and tramcars gave her a headache after having a whole river valley to herself. "The nights here are marvelous. Utterly silent."

Mary exulted in every detail of her new life, from her first dance to the first ride on her horse, Dan, bought for her by the local homesteaders. She loved "the clean sharp cold and the snow," and was awestruck by her first view of the northern lights, which she could see from every part of her shack. "Last night, I rode seven miles by the light of the northern lights . . . I was riding due south last night and the edge of them was in front of me and right over head was [a] wonderful sweep of coloured lights, pink and green. I got an awful crick in my neck from looking up all the time." To her, work was a gift, not a chore. Change was exhilarating, not frightening. "This is a great place. Life is extraordinarily interesting from scrubbing floors and cleaning windows to removing teeth for Red Indians. I'm enjoying every minute of it. I really do seem to fall on my feet."

Photographs of her taken during her first year in northern Alberta show a young woman with a clear gaze wearing a jacket, breeches and moccasins. She is clearly delighted to be where she is and has a fresh, happy demeanour. She was part of a new generation of women doctors who functioned on their own, without husband or family, in tough frontier practices.

A typical day for Mary might have involved riding her horse through tangled trails to a child sick with tuberculosis or a trapper who had missed a tree with his axe and inconveniently chopped his foot instead. She had to deliver a baby with pigs squealing under the bed. She monitored attacks of dysentery due to polluted well water, which during her long career she worked to amend. For this she was paid $160 a month and expected to work every day, 24 hours a day.

Over the years, Mary endured temperatures so cold in her shack she had to rise every two hours to stoke the fire to keep from freezing. The tea froze in the teapot; she had to thaw ink before writing a letter. Often she spent more time in the saddle than in her own bed. She survived everything, from innumerable falls into the river with her horse ("half the men in the area had to fish me out of the river at one time or another") to a nightmare sleigh ride to Peace River hospital with a man who had fractured his skull after the tree he was felling dropped on his head. "The old chap was in a terror on the way down. We traveled all night, did ninety miles fairly heavy sleighing (there was another 12 inches snowfall last week) in nineteen hours, thirteen hours driving and six hours rest, all with one team of horses . . . But he was difficult to look after, exceedingly irritable in spells, tried to get up and go for a walk! Would suddenly sit bolt upright on the camp bed. All this in a small tent on the top of a rocking sleigh and we had to have a stove inside the tent, of course. I was terrified that I should drowse off and he'd sit up and a jolt of the sleigh would send him headfirst onto the heater!" And so she and the sleigh driver forged on into the night, with "the little tent, lit up inside, looking a sort of glowing orange colour, crawling over mile after mile of snow, with the northern lights shimmering and swaying above us, pale apple-green and gold edged with mauve. It was a perfect night."

Another time, she nearly drowned while crossing Jack Knife Creek. Both of the bridges had been swept away in a flood. Yet she had to get to a patient on the other side. "So the horse got in but couldn't get a footing in the almost vertical wall of mud [on] the other side and nearly drowned me trying to, so we had to swim up stream and get out [on the] same side. Water was only up to my waist, of course, but rather chilly, as you can imagine, as the snow was still melting in the bush.

"So there I was, soaked to the waist, still on the wrong side of the creek!! Well, there was a man loading hay the other side, who had nearly drowned his team the day before, so he hauled my horse over with a rope, while I walked over on a couple of thin poplar poles, which incidentally rolled over and tipped me in again!! And then I had a four mile ride to Ashworths' in my wet clothes and the wind was from the east . . . I'm still enjoying it, in spite of minor mishaps like this!"

And she did love it, whether she was treating patients or settling into her armchair with her feet on the stove and a cup of hot cocoa in her hands, her gramophone playing and a copy of *Punch* magazine to read. She loved the independence of living solo and declined invitations to stay with the local Mountie and his wife.

Mary Percy was an unusual woman. She wasn't the doctor's wife, but the doctor. The wilderness had not become her home for lack of choices. She wanted to be there. She never speaks of being courageous, and yet she lived alone in her first years in Alberta, climbing on her horse in the vicious cold and riding through the night to visit the sick and the dying. The isolated community saw her as their hope—the travelling angel who was not above pitching in to help sick homesteaders with their chores. When a visiting nurse pointed out that in England, no nurse would cook or do housework, Mary wrote indignantly: "Well, well. If it isn't beneath my dignity as a doctor to turn in and scrub the floor or feed the pigs, I'm *damned* if I see why it should be beyond hers as a nurse to wash and feed 5 young children." No matter how bad it got, she claimed she wouldn't return to England "for a thousand dollars." She came to Alberta for a year and stayed forever.

Mary did not pine for a suitor. She attended dances, played bridge and thoroughly enjoyed a good laugh. But then someone appeared on her doorstep with a septic hand. Frank Jackson, an attractive widower with two small sons, lived farther north in Keg River. He started finding excuses to show up on her doorstep with patients from the north or with ducks for her dinner. Once, when the river was flooded, he hauled himself hand by hand over the raging torrent by telegraph wire to bring her one of his courtship presents: another duck. One night, she hauled out the heavy artillery, playing Puccini on the gramophone. "If you know of anything more calculated to entice a man, I don't know it. The man never had a chance!" she laughed in remembrance years later. In 1931, at the age of 27, Dr. Percy left her post at Battle River Prairie and moved north to Keg River to marry Frank Jackson. There, she became the unpaid doctor to the impoverished Metis, working to eradicate tuberculosis in her community. Mary was much honoured before her death in 2000. She was awarded an Honorary Doctor of Laws degree by the University of Alberta, named "Woman of the Year" in 1975 by the Voice of Native Women and presented with a Centennial Medal in 1967 and the Order of Canada in 1990. "One of the greatest challenges of general practice is to give a worthwhile life to those we keep alive," she said. "It calls for empathy as well as drugs." The lively medical graduate who leaped at the chance to become a doctor on horseback had a profound effect on generations of Native peoples and non-Natives in northern Alberta.

Even now, in the 21st century, how many young women would so lightheartedly move to an isolated cabin and take incredible risks to travel through subarctic weather on treacherous trails to visit infectious patients who in turn might infect them? Today, it would be an unusual, although not outrageous choice. In 1929, it was astounding.

CHAPTER

11

Gladys Reeves
(1890–1974)

"There were many, many times when I'd think I'd come to the end of my tether and just couldn't go on and then I'd be afraid. They'd say, 'I told you so.' And I'd start in again."

—GLADYS REEVES

GLADYS REEVES FOLLOWED HER CRAFT, her art and her passion—whether it was in her achievements as a pioneer in western photography, her relationship with legendary photographer Ernest Brown or her love of flowers, which led to her pioneering work with the Edmonton Horticultural Society.

Born in 1890 in Somerset, England, Gladys came to Edmonton with her family in 1904. At the age of 15, she walked into the studio of Ernest Brown, sent by her mother to inform him that her sister had turned down a job with him. Gladys was offered a job as a receptionist in the office, which evolved into an apprenticeship with the historic photographer.·

The studio was so cold in the Alberta winter that "no amount of heat could keep the studio warm, and I had to put bricks in the stove to put under my feet while I sat retouching photographs. Mr. Brown came in one day and was very put out because his cigar had frozen in his mouth."

Five years later, she had her own studio, The Art League. "I started my own studio in 1920. I had the unfortunate position of being a woman. And in those days a woman was not recognized. I think I was the first woman west of Portage La Prairie to start a photographic studio on my own." It was one thing to work as a photographer in a studio owned by a seasoned photographer; it was quite another for a woman to own her own facility. She worked with an eight-by-ten-inch camera with glass plates, primitive by today's standards, and specialized in portraiture.

When her studio burned in 1929, destroying not only her work but also the archived negatives of her mentor and lifelong friend Ernest Brown, she recovered and established a new studio above the Empress Theatre on Jasper Avenue in downtown Edmonton, with Brown's assistance. She maintained it until 1950. An advertisement for the studio, surrounded by ads for the City Telephone System and a lumber company, reads in part, "The Value of Photographs

Gladys Reeves was a pioneering woman photographer and the first female president of the Edmonton Horticultural Society. In this photograph taken around 1915, she stands next to her camera and tripod. PROVINCIAL ARCHIVES OF ALBERTA A14076.

is in the Future. The Key to our Endeavours is Permanency."
Below this is "Gladys Reeves" in large print, over "The Art
League Studio" in smaller print. So much has been written
of Gladys' devotion to Ernest Brown that it is refreshing to
see her confidence in showcasing her name over that of her
studio.

In the 1930s, in addition to her own photographic work,
she worked with Brown, co-managing a museum called Birth
of the West. Eventually, the truckloads of dinosaur bones,
Native artifacts and thousands of photographs in the museum's collections were purchased by the Province of Alberta.

Although Gladys Reeves was devoted to Ernest Brown,
her elder, her mentor and, according to most sources, her
lover, her own achievements as a photographer were considerable. In 1938, her work was recognized at an international
exhibition in Chicago, where she placed in the top 10. To
maintain a photographic studio requires considerable skill,
and Gladys Reeves obviously maintained a reputation that
drew clients. Indubitably, her association with Brown was
beneficial, but ultimately, her work would stand on its own.

Ernest Brown and Gladys worked together successfully
and thrived in the boom years from 1904 to 1914, when portraiture was popular and Edmonton was expanding. When
the First World War changed fortunes and families, Brown's
services were less in demand. Nevertheless, The Art League
survived, while Brown retired to Vegreville.

Gladys Reeves was not only a photographer of merit,

she also left her mark on the city of Edmonton as the first female president of the Edmonton Horticultural Society. To be the first female president of any organization is a landmark event, but only those who have trod that path can understand the stress and adversity that a woman encounters in this situation. In the 1920s, women were more likely to be homemakers than heads of associations. Her public speeches as president were tributes to the joys of gardening. She viewed tree planting as a civic duty and was a strong advocate of the City Beautiful Movement. According to the Canadian Encyclopedia, the City Beautiful Movement promoted the planned creation of civic beauty through "architectural harmony, unified design and visual variety." It flourished in the 1890s and 1900s, with the underlying belief that beauty on the streets affected the common good and created a harmonious social environment.

Gladys was a key player in the planting of 5,000 trees in boulevards in Edmonton in 1923, through the Edmonton Tree Planting Committee. Her other interests included the Old Timers Association, the Friendship Club and the Soroptimist Society, which promotes social justice and equality and the empowerment of women. She sang in choirs, participated in early opera and the Alberta Music Festivals and arranged musical events at the horticultural society's garden shows. Her tremendous energy and appreciation of so many facets of society were a testimony to her lively spirit.

Her passion didn't stop at plants, the arts or photography. With Ernest Brown, she created a project of "teaching pictures" for schoolchildren. An extremely clever combination of commerce and education, the program was comprised of 31 series of historic photos divided into subject areas and accompanied by lessons and questions. Smaller cards were created for individual sale to schoolchildren.

If Gladys resented the somewhat chauvinistic attitude of Brown, a singular man of Victorian whiskers and bearing who inexplicably invited her, as his lover, to tea with his family, she never made it apparent in her public demeanour. She frequently took photographs of subjects and scenes photographed years before by Ernest Brown, almost as if she were revisiting the scenes and viewing them through her own, more mature eyes. She devoted many of her later years to being the custodian of Brown's work, cataloguing the Ernest Brown Collection for the Provincial Archives of Alberta and giving illustrated lectures to schools about his work.

Decades later, in 2009, an acclaimed theatre production, *The Unmarried Wife*, was produced by MAA and PAA Theatre in Edmonton and the Provincial Archives of Alberta. The title was drawn from a quote from Ernest Brown: "For today and forever, you will be my unmarried wife."

However, Gladys' devotion to Brown and his work should not overshadow her considerable achievements as a woman who did not follow the usual path. The conscripted arc of her youth should have sent her straight into the role of chatelaine, homemaker and helpmate. Perhaps she was the latter, but she never adopted the mantle of a woman who quietly maintained a home while sublimating her personality to that of the man in her life. Gladys Reeves made her mark as a photographer in her own right.

As a very young girl, she had the courage and sense of adventure to accept a job as an assistant in a profession that was unusual at the time. She struck out and opened her own photographic studio when women did not do such things. Her contemporaries, except for the rare flappers and art deco society girls, were mostly content to live at home under the safe umbrella of their families. Gladys chose to follow her own path. She survived the destruction of her studio, then rebuilt. She leaves a lasting legacy through her custodianship of the Ernest Brown Collection, her own work and the tree-lined streets of Edmonton today, which are a visual tribute to her foresight and determination.

Gladys died in 1974 at the age of 83, leaving behind her a city made more beautiful by her presence.

12

Winnifred Eaton
(1875–1954)

"Strip her of her glittering clothes, put her in rags over a wash-tub, and she would have been transformed into a common thing. But I? If you put me over a wash-tub, I tell you I would have woven a romance, aye, from the very suds. God had planted in me the fairy germs; that I knew."

—WINNIFRED EATON IN
ME, A BOOK OF REMEMBRANCE

THIS WAS THE SURVIVAL TACTIC of Winnifred Eaton. No matter what happened to the woman who was born into poverty in Montreal to English and Chinese parents at a time when interracial marriages were considered socially deviant, she changed like a chameleon and created a world that suited her.

Winnifred was a working girl at the turn of the 20th century. While earning a living as a reporter in Jamaica, then as a typist in the stockyards of Chicago, she churned out stories at night, dreaming of fame. A hugely successful romantic novelist under the pseudonym Onoto Watanna, Winnifred became a New York celebrity and a Hollywood screenwriter. After a failed marriage and a disappointing Broadway debut as a playwright, she recreated herself once more, establishing herself in the Canadian literary community.

Winnifred Eaton's mother may have been the only Chinese woman residing in Montreal in the late 1800s. Her father was English, an artist, and unable to provide adequately for his 14 children. Winnifred's options at the time were minimal. Half-caste, impoverished, a woman—surely her best hope was becoming a laundress or a maid. Instead, she escaped from that scenario as soon as possible, at the tender age of 20. She had no training, but the publication of a poem in a local paper led to a job offer from the publisher of *Galls News Letter* in Kingston, Jamaica. He frequently hired young Canadian women "to do virtually all the work of running his newspaper." This was the start of a literary career for Winnifred.

Later, while working as a typist in Chicago, Winnifred wrote poetic stories about delicate Japanese ladies to satisfy commercial tastes and make some extra money. Her early novels, which at first glance could be dismissed as romantic reading, nevertheless featured unconventional heroines trying to overcome social challenges by using their brains as much as their beauty. They were a huge success. *A Japanese Nightingale*, published in 1901, sold over 200,000 copies, a huge coup for an author in that era. It was made into a silent film and also a Broadway play.

Mercurial and inventive, Winnifred recreated her history and always chose drama over accuracy. The need to escape was partly due to denial, or at least a cloaking, of her racial background. Winnifred rarely acknowledged her Chinese blood, yet she adopted a Japanese *nom de plume*, Onoto Watanna, for her incredibly successful novels and posed for publicity photos in Japanese costume. She was an intriguing and exotic figure to New York society in the early 1900s, and her mystique served her well.

Part of Winnifred's talent was in constantly recreating herself. In her thinly disguised autobiography, *Me, A Book of Remembrance*, Winnifred describes her journey from reporter to typist to writer, taking some liberties with the truth. The anonymous book created such a sensation when it was published in 1915 that New York subway advertisements asked, "Who is the author of *ME*?"

The writer never doubted her uniqueness. "I had always secretly believed there were the strains of genius somewhere hidden in me: I had always lived in a little dream world of my own, wherein, beautiful and courted I moved among the elect of the earth." If she ever wavered in confidence, she regrouped and surged back with the instinct of a survivor. Years later, in her 1920s novel *Movie Madness*, she wrote, "If one has imagination he can really get out of himself— escape from the common everyday sordid things in life." And so she did.

Winnifred wrote magazine articles, memoirs, screenplays and novels. She did it all and she did it well. Nevertheless, supporting three children while suffering through a divorce from her first husband, reporter Bertrand Babcock, wore on her. In the unpublished "You Can't Run Away From Yourself," she remembered, "Writing became a sort of torment—something I had literally to drive myself to. Many a time I have laid my head down among my papers and pencils and cried—hopelessly, for there seemed no escape for me. There were many dependent upon me."

Her escape route came in the person of Frank Reeve. They met in Reno, while awaiting their respective divorces to be finalized. "He was a big fellow, the kind one calls a man's man. His personality emanated a dominating, fine, clean sort of strength. He had steady, keen, kind blue eyes and a strong chin." Her children loved him. Winnifred balked at first at his marriage proposal, saying she wanted to stay free and hoping that the promise of work in the film industry would materialize. Frank was persuasive. She recalled his pitch: "Why write love stories. Live one. Let's cut all this out. Marry me, and we will go out west—northwest—out to some big country—a country in the making! What do you say?" They were married in Connecticut in 1917 and moved to a ranch near Calgary, Alberta.

Frank and Winnifred were opposites. He was business-like, straightforward and methodical. She was emotional, impulsive and hopeless with money. He loved her. In her way, she must have loved him.

While she lived with Frank in Alberta, Winnifred wrote the novel *Cattle*. It was a deliberate departure from the style of writing that had made her famous. *Cattle* is rough and rather crudely written, with the larger-than-life characters brawling against the backdrop of the Alberta scenery. In 1924, she had decided to wield "a stronger pen" and create a novel that matched the magnificent landscape around her. "I made up my mind I would not go back to Japanese stories. I would start all over again, with a new pseudonym and a new type of writing. I would write of the great ranching country—the last of the big lands—where I had sojourned for so long. I had a passionate desire to send out into the world a living picture of Alberta. My former work had been chiefly noted for its delicate and even poetic quality . . . But I was not going to write with a delicate pen now." Although *Cattle* received mixed reviews, many felt it was worthy of consideration as a significant early Canadian novel.

Winnifred captured the Alberta landscape vividly. In her narrative, she reflected her surroundings and perhaps her own eagerness for respite from her churning life: "Alberta is, in a way, a land of sanctuary, and upon its rough

Winnifred Eaton Reeve at her ranch, located west of Calgary, sometime in the 1920s. GLENBOW ARCHIVES NA-4320-9

bosom the derelicts of the world, the fugitive, the hunted, the sick and the dying have sought asylum and cure." This time, instead of creating delicate Japanese women, Winnifred opted for physically intimidating characters like Angella, the formidable Englishwoman who is the only person capable of keeping the villain at bay.

Winters in Alberta were hard. Being cooped up was foreign and disconcerting to Winnifred. The isolation of living on a ranch took its toll, and Winnifred rented a house in Calgary the next winter. "It wasn't that I wanted so much to return to New York and my friends—but deep inside me was the overpowering urge—to write! I realized that when I went down to Calgary, shut myself in a room for two weeks, and it seemed as if I had turned on a mental faucet. Everything wanted to come tumbling out of me at once!"

Winnifred could never be a conventional western wife. Although she put up a good façade, it was not in her nature to pickle vegetables or work outdoors. Above all, she was a writer, and although she claimed not to have great talent, she had a rich imagination and the skills to put it to use in commercial form. "Something beat like an aching pulse away back in my mind and deep in my heart. Letters from New York thrilled me to the bone. I could have hugged a stranger from out of my old world. And then my work— my writing!" She felt trapped. Her money was tied up with Frank's in their property, and Frank was happy in Alberta. But Winnifred yearned for more.

Under some financial duress, Frank and Winnifred ended up selling the ranch, and in 1924, Frank took a job in a stockbrokerage firm on the Calgary Exchange. In Calgary, Winnifred was unable to generate the income that she could elsewhere, and life there palled. After being trapped indoors for three weeks by a vicious storm, she knew she had to leave. So, despite Frank's misgivings, but with his best wishes, she and the three children returned to New York in the hope of resurrecting her writing career, possibly in motion pictures.

Winnifred had a flurry of interviews with film companies. Friends rallied to recommend her, and she appeared to be on the brink of yet another career breakthrough. Yet Frank wrote to her, asking her to return. She responded: "How could I live in Alberta and go on with my work? Today most women work—married or single . . . My business is as important as yours and yours as important as mine and neither of us can sacrifice his interests for the other."

After a few months in New York, Universal Pictures offered Winnifred a job in Hollywood as scenario editor-in-chief. This was a powerful position, but not unusual for the motion-picture industry in the 1920s, when there were many successful women writers. What made it extraordinary was her age: she was in her 50s. Winnifred had a significant body of work behind her, including 15 books, most of them bestsellers. Now, she was about to embark on a phase of her career where she would have to work to tight deadlines on screenplays, screen treatments, synopses and story ideas. It was a great opportunity and a coup for the resilient but at times forgotten writer. In the next few years, she wrote dozens of screenplays, including *Shanghai Lady* and *Mississippi Gambler*. She so impressed Carl Laemmle Sr., the founder of Universal Pictures, that he wired to his employees on the west coast: "HAVE CONFIDENCE IN MRS. REEVE CONSIDER SHE HAS SHOWN GREATEST ABILITY ANY EDITOR YET."

Yet Winnifred fretted. "When I was in Hollywood, my own personality reacted against me. I found myself holding an executive position in a world of seething politics. I was constitutionally unable to handle my problem and made enemies . . . I had in fact everything that should have made me valuable to a film company. They needed story brains— and I had them. They needed imagination, and that I had; but I did not have a pinch of tact . . . desperate and alienated from my husband, I sold my things for anything I could get immediately."

Winnifred's Hollywood career became more stressful when she had to fight for every credit and every piece of work. One of her screenplays, *What Men Want*, was produced by Universal Studios in 1930 without crediting her as writer, which must have been galling to a woman to whom recognition was paramount. She worked on hundreds of stories and scripts, but typically for that time in Hollywood history, she is credited with only six screenplays. Years later in an interview, she reflected, "Yes, I made something of a name for myself in Hollywood, but the fame of a film writer is very ephemeral."

When she sensed that her footing in Hollywood was becoming shaky, Winnifred embarked on a campaign to win back Frank. She knew they were a well-matched couple, and he was now financially secure once more. In future years, Frank would become an extremely wealthy man. He and two friends owned a lease in Turner Valley, the site of major oil discoveries in the 1930s, a lease that guaranteed them financial security for the rest of their lives. Although reportedly never ceasing to love the absent Winnifred, Frank had acquired a mistress. Winnifred seethed when she heard her replacement had possession of some of her most beloved personal treasures, including a signed first edition of Mark Twain's *A Connecticut Yankee in King Arthur's Court*.

By the early 1930s, Winnifred was ready to leave Hollywood. She had been laid off by Universal and was determined to rebuild her life with Frank. Yet Frank was not breaking any speed records in splitting up with his lady friend. As always, she used her creative powers to overcome her feelings of despair. She wrote an unsigned story about her relationship with Frank and his lover called "Because We Were Lonely" and sold it to *True Story Magazine*. She wrote it, amazingly, from the viewpoint of the other woman. Winnifred was full of surprises. She never did the expected.

Eventually, Frank and Winnifred reconciled, and she

returned to Alberta. This time she stayed, becoming very active in the Calgary branch of the Canadian Authors Association. She was also a founding member of the Little Theatre Association in Calgary and an active and influential member of the creative community as a whole. The Reeve Theatre at the University of Calgary is named in her honour.

She died in Montana in 1954, while returning from California with Frank.

Winnifred was a powerful creative force. Early in her career, she wrote, "My work showed always the effect of my life—my lack of training, my poor preparation for the business of writing, my dense ignorance. I can truly say of my novels that they are strangely like myself, unfulfilled promises." But this certainly was not true later in her life. She had underestimated her creative powers, for her novels are enduring and are finding a cult following 100 years after she wrote them. The life of Winnifred Eaton Babcock Reeve is a lesson in survival and creativity. She was unique. She was a survivor. She was a rebel.

Bibliography

Andrews, D. Larraine. *The Cowboy Trail: A Guide to Alberta's Historic Cowboy Country*. Calgary: Brindle & Glass, 2006.

Armatage, Kay. *The Girl from God's Country: Nell Shipman and the Silent Cinema*. Toronto: University of Toronto Press, 2003.

Binnie-Clark, Georgina. *Wheat and Woman*. Toronto: Bell and Cockburn, 1914. Reprint, Toronto: University of Toronto Press, 1979.

Birchall, Diana. *Onoto Watanna: The Story of Winnifred Eaton*. Champaign: University of Illinois Press, 2001.

Bolus, Malvina. "The Son of I. Gunn." *The Beaver* (Winter 1971):23–26.

Brennan, Brian. *Scoundrels and Scallywags: Characters from Alberta's Past*. Calgary: Fifth House Publishers, 2002.

Cook, Sharon Anne, Lorna R. McLean, and Kate O'Rourke. *Framing Our Past: Canadian Women's History in the Twentieth Century*. Montreal and Kingston: McGill-Queen's University Press, 2001.

Coues, Elliott, ed. *New Light on the Early History of the Greater Northwest: The Manuscript Journals of Alexander Henry and of David Thompson*. 3 vols. New York: Francis P. Harper, 1897. Reprint, Minneapolis: Ross & Haines, 1965.

Eaton, Winnifred. *Me, A Book of Remembrance*. New York: Century Company, 1915. Reprint, Jackson: University Press of Mississippi, 1997.

Edmonton Horticultural Society. www.edmontonhort.com/about/history/php.

Foster, Merna. *100 Canadian Heroines: Famous and Forgotten Faces*. Toronto: Dundurn Press, 2004.

Gowan, Bruce. *Wings over Calgary 1906–1940*. Calgary: Chinook Country Chapter, Alberta Historical Society, 1990.

Hacker, Carlotta. *The Indomitable Lady Doctors*. Toronto: Clarke, Irwin & Co., 1974. Reprint, Halifax: Formac Publishing Co., 2001.

Harper, Kenn. "Taissumani: A Day in Arctic History, Nov. 2, 1860—A Fortuitous Meeting." *Nunatsiaq News*, October 28, 2005.

Jackel, Susan. *A Flannel Shirt and Liberty: British Emigrant Gentlewomen in the Canadian West, 1880–1914*. Vancouver: University of British Columbia Press, 1982.

Jackson, Mary Percy. *Suitable for the Wilds: Letters from Northern Alberta, 1929–31*. Edited by Janice Dickin McGinnis. Toronto: University of Toronto Press, 1995.

LeCompte, Mary Lou. *Cowgirls of the Rodeo: Pioneer Professional Athletes*. Urbana: University of Illinois Press, 1993.

Lehn, Cornelia. *The Homemade Brass Plate*. Sardis, BC: Cedar-Cott Enterprise, 1988.

Leishman, McNeill. *Tales of the Old Town*. Calgary: Calgary Herald, 1966.

Livingstone, Donna. *The Cowboy Spirit: Guy Weadick and the Calgary Stampede*. Vancouver: Greystone Books, 1996.

Loomis, Chauncey. "Arctic Profiles: Ebierbing (ca. 1887–ca. 1881)," http://pubs.aina.ucalgary.ca/arctic/Arctic39-2-186.pdf.

MacEwan, Grant. . . . *And Mighty Women Too*. Saskatoon: Western Producer Prairie Books, 1975.

Morris, Peter. *Embattled Shadows: A History of Canadian Cinema, 1895–1939*. Montreal and Kingston: McGill-Queen's University Press, 1992.

National Film Board. *Wanted! Doctor on Horseback*. Film, 1996.

Nickerson, Sheila. *Midnight to the North: The Untold Story of the Inuit Woman Who Saved the Polaris Expedition*. New York: Jeremy P. Tarcher/Putnam, 2002.

Bibliography

Peach, Jack. *Thanks for the Memories*. Saskatoon: Fifth House Publishers, 1994.

Pigott, Peter. *Flying Canucks: Famous Canadian Aviators*. Toronto: Hounslow Press, 1996.

Robinson, Roxana. *Georgia O'Keeffe*. Hanover, NH: University Press of New England, 1999.

Rogers, Will. *The Papers of Will Rogers: Volume Two, Wild West and Vaudeville, April 1904–September 1908*. Edited by Arthur Frank Wertheim and Barbara Bair. Norman: University of Oklahoma Press, 2000.

Shipman, Nell. *The Silent Screen and My Talking Heart*. Boise: Boise State University, 1987.

Smith, Cyndi. *Off the Beaten Track: Women Adventurers and Mountaineers in Western Canada*. Jasper, AB: Coyote Books, 1989.

Van Kirk, Sylvia. *Many Tender Ties, Women in Fur Trade Society in Western Canada, 1670–1870*. Winnipeg: Watson & Dyer, 1980.

Wachowich, Nancy, "Taqulittuq," www.jrank.org/history/pages/8163/Taqulittuq-(-Hannah-Tookoolito-c-1839-%E2%80%93-76-)-Ipirvik-(-Joe-Ebierbing-Eskimo-Joe-c-1839-%E2%80%93-c-1881-).html.

Walker, Joseph, and Juanita Walker. *The Light on Her Face*. Hollywood: ASC Press, 1984.

Wheelwright, Julie. *Amazons and Military Maids: Women Who Dressed as Men in Pursuit of Life, Liberty and Happiness*. London: Pandora, 1989.

Whyte, Jon. *Lake Louise, A Diamond in the Wilderness*. Photographs compiled and edited by Carole Harmon. Banff: Altitude Publishing, 1982.

Winegarten, Debra L. *Katherine Stinson: The Flying Schoolgirl*. New York: Eakin Press, 2000.

Index

Index

Acknowledgements

What would writers of biography and history do without archives, museums and public libraries? These are the resources that preserve our heritage and allow the writer to forage for facts on sometimes obscure subjects. Thank heavens for the helpful and patient staff at the Glenbow Archives, where I perused and pondered *The Canadian Alpine Journal*, *The Farm and Ranch Review* and other publications that were like buried treasure. Equal blessing must be bestowed on Special Collections, University of Calgary Library, where I revelled in the Winnifred Eaton Reeve fonds and disturbed the serene hush of the room by laughing out loud at Georgina Binnie-Clark's *A Summer on the Canadian Prairie*. Apollonia Steele never once looked at me disapprovingly, despite my unladylike chuckles, and for that, and for locating the innumerable fonds I requested, I thank her.

Yvonne Snider-Nighswander, archivist of the Hudson's Bay Company Archives at the Provincial Archives of Manitoba, offered extraordinary assistance by sending a gold mine of information on the elusive Isabel Gunn, and doing it with generous care and incredible speed. The Provincial Archives of Alberta were one of the few sources of details on the life of Gladys Reeves that I discovered. As I say, archives and archivists are a wonderful national resource and we should treat them nicely.

I don't know the names of the librarians at the Calgary Public Library who assisted me in the Local History Room, but I have to say they were very helpful, and the room itself was so lovely, filled with great, precious, out-of-print books, that I wanted to pitch a tent and stay there forever. I urge all and sundry to get a library card and explore the wonderful resources of the library. I discovered books through the online search catalogue, like Joseph and Juanita Walker's *The Light on Her Face*, that I would never have known about otherwise.

Acknowledgements

I send heartfelt thanks to Kory Baker-Henderson of Great North Productions in Edmonton, who packed together a huge file of Nell Shipman research from Boise State University as well as a copy of *The Silent Screen and My Talking Heart* (that I had ordered from Amazon.com and which never arrived, which is a great argument for sticking close to home when you need information). Many thanks to Alan Virta of Boise State University Library for his gracious response to our request for photographs. I also thank Brian Dooley and George Williams of Great North Productions, who sent me a copy of the award-winning documentary *Ah gee, forgetting me . . . Nell Shipman*, a lovely work that makes you want to run out into the streets and shout Nell Shipman's name for all to hear and celebrate.

Writers are a wonderful bunch. When they hear another writer needs help with research, they pitch right in. That is what Debra Winegarten in Texas did when I contacted her. She sent me a copy of her wonderful book *Katherine Stinson, the Flying Schoolgirl,* which I found inspiring and informative and from which I shamelessly filched details of Katherine's amazing life. Thank you, Debra, for that and for the enthusiastic words of encouragement.

Diana Birchall, the granddaughter and biographer of Winnifred Eaton in *Onoto Watanna: The Story of Winnifred Eaton*, and I embarked on an energetic email correspondence, in which Diana constantly encouraged my work and offered insights into the process of writing biography. She is a true find as a writer, correspondent and fellow artist.

There are so many fine books from which I have harvested quotes, anecdotes and details that I fret that I have may have overlooked some. If so, please forgive the oversight. It is the fault of being overloaded with wonderful resources, not by intent. (As other writers have confessed, I was hunting down additional information even in the last moments and wondering if I had time to work the great new tidbits into the chapters.) I have acknowledged many sources in the bibliography, but would particularly like to recognize the following: the terrific articles on Nell Shipman by Kay Armatage, which I found on the Internet; Susan Jackel's wonderful work in *A Flannel Shirt and Liberty*; the journals of Alexander Henry (the Younger), *New Light on the Early History of the*

Greater Northwest, edited by Elliott Coues (even though Mr. Henry isn't around anymore to thank, one must be grateful to people who took the trouble to keep a journal so that the rest of us can have a clue about historic events); the impeccably detailed article in the winter 1971 issue of *The Beaver* by Malvina Bolus, which may be the definitive word on Isabel Gunn; the scholarly work *Framing Our Past*, by Sharon Anne Cook, Lorna R. McLean and Kate O'Rourke, which is a national treasure in terms of defining women's place in the history of Canada; *Tales of the Old Town* by McNeill Leishman; *Scoundrels and Scallywags* by Brian Brennan; *Wings over Calgary 1906–1940* by Bruce Gowan; *The Indomitable Lady Doctors* by Carlotta Hacker; the intriguing work of Julie Wheelwright in *Amazons and Military Maids*; the incredible detail in *Many Tender Ties, Women in Fur Trade Society in Western Canada, 1670–1870* by Sylvia Van Kirk; *Thanks for the Memories* by Jack Peach, . . . *And Mighty Women Too* by Grant McEwan; *Embattled Shadows* by Peter Morris, which offers some of the definitive Shipman stories; *Flying Canucks* by Peter Pigott; *Georgia O'Keeffe* by Roxana Robinson, which offered some wonderful insights into the young Georgia Engelhard (and which I found in my favourite second-hand bookstore); the fabulous *Off the Beaten Track* by Cyndi Smith, which I recommend to anybody who loves mountains and mountaineers; the lovely National Film Board video *Wanted! Doctor on Horseback*, which makes you want to leap into the screen and kiss Mary Percy Jackson; *The Homemade Brass Plate*, with more delightful quotes from Mary Percy, as told to Cornelia Lehn; and so many more works that offered insights into the lives of the rebel women.

More thanks galore to Donna Livingstone, the erudite and joyous soul who started it all, Shirley Render, the Canadian 99's, Brian Brennan, all the people who responded to my calls for help with research, and with love, to my fellow rebels in the Calgary creative community.

Writing is a lonely business. Then the editor steps in. It is very handy to have landed an editor who is smart, sensitive and considerate. I got lucky and found Kara Turner. Thank you, Kara, for your informed and very nicely put suggestions. The second time around, for this expanded edition of *Rebel Women*, I was fortunate to work with Lesley Reynolds, who is patient and meticulous beyond words.

Acknowledgements

Mostly, I thank the rebel women who wrote their words for posterity. Georgina Binnie-Clark in *Wheat and Woman*, Nell Shipman in *The Silent Screen and My Talking Heart*, Winnifred Eaton in *Me, A Book of Remembrance* and Mary Percy Jackson in *Suitable for the Wilds* gave us the great gift of their own words. I am deeply grateful that their voices were not silenced.

And finally, thank you to my family who think what I do is worthwhile, instead of a big nuisance. Thank you for your support, Aunt Betty, my cousins Michael, Deb, Randy and Donna, and my darling mother, Julia.

About the Author

Linda Kupecek is an award-winning author, journalist and screen-writer. A graduate in drama from the University of Alberta, she has acted in numerous film and theatre productions, including the classic film *McCabe* and *Mrs. Miller*. Her books cover many genres, including historical nonfiction, mystery and humour. Her writing has been featured in publications such as *The Hollywood Reporter*, *City Palate* and *TV Guide*, and she often appears as a lifestyle columnist on CBC radio and television. She lives in Calgary, Alberta.

More Great Books in the Amazing Stories Series

A preview of

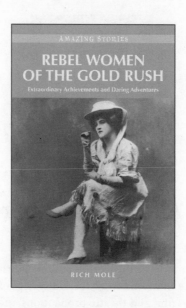

During the frenzied Klondike Gold Rush, many daring women
ventured north to seek riches and adventure or to escape a troubled
past. These unforgettable, strong-willed women defied the social
conventions of the time and endured heartbreak and horrific
conditions to build a life in the wild North. From renowned reporter
Faith Fenton and successful entrepreneur Belinda Mulrooney to Mae
Field, "The Doll of Dawson," the Klondike's rebel women bring an
intriguing new perspective to gold-rush history.

print ISBN 978-1-894974-76-9
ebook ISBN 978-1-926613-88-8

Visit heritagehouse.ca to see the entire list of books in this series.

8

Making Their Way

AS ETHEL BERRY AND HER sister discovered, "women's work" began even before reaching the Klondike. Della Banks and her prospector husband, Thompson, were among the first wave of gold seekers to hit the trail in 1897. It wasn't the first time Della had accompanied Thompson on his "perennial search for fortune," so she knew what to expect. Like Emily Craig, Della Banks realized cooking along the trail would fall to her. What was different for Della was that her husband and his companions agreed to pay her for the work. However, she found the money barely compensated for the working conditions.

"I got supper in the rain by the light of a candle," she related over 40 years later. The memories of it all still rankled. "Kneeling on the ground, I mixed biscuits—90 of them, baked fifteen at a time in the sheet-iron stove. Thompson watched, saying that if he had to get supper that night, there wouldn't be any. Well," Della snorted, "I had walked as far as he had."

After surviving the arduous journey to the land of the midnight sun, work began in earnest. Many women had come to the Klondike in search of financial freedom and independence. For those who expected to dig up gold and go home rich, the first few days in Dawson City and on the creeks were a painful shock. Even for 1897's first arrivals, there were few claims left to stake.

For most, finding work—at least, legitimate work away from Paradise Alley—proved almost impossible. However, for those who could overcome the fear and fatigue, there were opportunities waiting.

Cashing in on the Masculine Market

Soon after tents were raised along Dawson City's riverbank, women found financial success, opening businesses such as restaurants, laundries and baths, where many men parted with their gold in return for goods and services.

Anna DeGraf hefted a sewing machine across the Chilkoot more than once. She never lacked work, sewing furs for Jack McQuesten's A.C. Company in Circle City and then, during Dawson's heyday, sewing costumes for the dance-hall girls at the Orpheum Theatre. She also created cold-weather clothes for the NWMP. At one time, Anna employed at least four other women in her workshop. The widow was far too busy to contemplate marriage, although she received at least two proposals. Anna was also successful at staking many claims. She received numerous tips about open claims and would stealthily wander up the creeks in the dead of night to hammer in her stakes before competitors arrived at dawn.

Having left Seattle, Frances Dorley was determined to stay in the North. After three months of searching, she found a cabin near Grand Forks, at the junction of Bonanza and Eldorado creeks. She converted the building into a roadhouse for weary travellers. "I baked tons of bread and pies and made millions of doughnuts," she recalled. Butter arrived in five-pound wooden buckets. Once emptied of butter, Frances filled them with baked beans.

By spring, Frances was back in Dawson City and had reacquainted herself with a certain Mrs. Moore, a middle-aged southern widow she had met at Lake Bennett the year before. The two women entered a partnership, and their Professional Men's Boarding House became a rip-roaring success.

As she had done in so many other gold camps, Nellie Cashman turned to food service for income and opened Dawson's Can-Can in the early summer of 1898. By the fall, she had opened the Cassiar Restaurant and had also operated a store. Cashman's lasting fame came from her philanthropy. Her legendary generosity began years earlier in BC, where she provided tender care to prospectors who gave her the nickname "Angel of the Cassiar." A few weeks after arriving in the Klondike, Nellie was walking the creeks, asking prospectors to dig deep for an expansion to St. Mary's Hospital.

A tender-hearted woman, Nellie looked and sounded like a tough-talking gold-field veteran. Her relationship with prospectors was unique. "Men are a nuisance," she complained good-naturedly to an interviewer. "Men— why, child, they're just boys grown up. I've nursed them, embalmed them, fed and scolded them, acted as mother confessor and fought my own with them and you have to treat them just like boys."

Kate Ryan was perhaps the best-known restaurateur on the Stikine Trail. Initially, the former nurse fed members of the NWMP and later opened a Glenora restaurant. After two years of travel, Kate arrived in Canada's newest railway town, Whitehorse, where she opened Kate's Café. Here, her life turned in an unusual direction.

Soon after her arrival, the NWMP called on Kate to take a job as prison matron. Gold smuggling had become a concern, and the Canadian government required a female gold inspector. Formidable-looking Kate was the only serious candidate for the position. She accepted a post as woman special constable, designed her own uniform and began riding the trains and the steamers, asking passengers if they had any gold to declare.

On board a steamer docked at Whitehorse, Constable

Ryan's question was greeted by indignant silence from one fashionable woman. Kate repeated the question, but to no avail. "I'm sorry, madam, but if you do not answer the questions, you will have to be searched."

"Oh, scarcely," came the haughty reply. "Do you know to whom you are speaking? I am the wife of Major General Gerald Brompton of the United States Army."

"And I, madam, am myself an officer of the British Crown. Would you kindly step into the cabin?"

Moments later, the woman had literally let down her hair, reluctantly exposing a number of concealed nuggets.

There were big profits to be made on Dawson City's seamy side. Within four months of her arrival from the Australian gold fields, unorthodox Marguerite Laimee opened the first of two Dawson cigar stores, which were merely fronts for bawdy houses. Traffic was so good that she poured $30 of gold into her pokes each morning from floor sweepings. The "stores" grossed $60,000 in less than two years. With the profits, Marguerite purchased a prime half-acre city lot for just $750 and quickly leased it for $500 a month. But her biggest financial windfall was yet to come.

Women of the Creeks

The few women who made their way north to the confluence of the Yukon and Klondike rivers shared the fate of most male stampeders: they were too late to stake claims. Those who did become prospectors either purchased claims from others or invested in a share of working prospects. Most of these women had much more profitable—and less contentious—sources of revenue.

Nellie Cashman invested her restaurant returns in claims, but was soon beset with legal disputes. The most serious allegation was that Nellie had tried to bribe Belinda Mulrooney by threatening to reveal information about Belinda's business associations with the mining inspector. Commissioner William Ogilvie was forced to investigate, and Nellie confessed she had been in error. Her obvious record of community work stood her in good stead, and no charges were laid.

Nellie struck it big with 19 below (the first, or "discovery" claim) on Bonanza Creek. She eventually bought out her partners and carted away more than $100,000 of ore. The proceeds bought her some less profitable claims, which she travelled to on snowshoes or by her dog team.

By the spring of 1899, Martha Purdy had managed to stake some claims on lesser-known Excelsior Creek. Within a few months, the claims were worth tens of thousands of dollars, and Martha, her brother and two partners were employing a crew of 16 to work them. She not only managed the businesses, but their kitchen too, cooking for all the men.

By 1901, Martha's family moved north to the Klondike from the US. They brought to Dawson the latest in mining technology—a mill to process ore and a hydraulic "monitor," and equipment to start a sawmill. The monitor's high-pressure jets of water left no gold concealed on Martha's holdings at her original mining claims. Soon, business was booming at the sawmill as well; money was rolling in, but success brought problems.

Martha took over lumber marketing after firing her salesman because of drunkenness. By the following spring, the sawmill foreman decided that he "wasn't gonna be run by a skirt." Equipment was sabotaged and the foreman was the primary suspect. When sabotage failed to stop production, the foreman coerced the men to pull out and incited the workers to stage a dramatic showdown in Martha's office. Purdy called their bluff, wrote out the men's final cheques and ordered the foreman off the property. When the foreman's public threats against Martha Purdy continued, the Mounties bluntly advised him to leave the Klondike.

"I'll get that hellcat yet!" the malcontent screamed as he shoved off from the wharf. Some days later when he entered American territory, a sheriff, perhaps tipped off by the NWMP, was waiting with a long-standing warrant and took him into custody. Meanwhile, "hellcat" Purdy kept on making "plenty of money," which allowed her to "buy the most beautiful clothes." It had been a long, hard struggle—"tough sledding," she called it—since her days as a separated pregnant mother struggling up the Trail of '98.

For legal advice, Martha turned to fellow Klondiker

and lawyer George Black. In the course of conversation, the lawyer mentioned that he was interested in becoming a politician and also suggested he was interested in something else—marriage to Martha. Two weeks after that initial legal consultation, George Black proposed. Martha admitted there was much to recommend the match (George Black and her boys hit it off almost immediately), but perhaps remembering her earlier, ill-fated marriage, Martha stated, "For once in my life, I let my head govern my heart." If George were serious, he would be patient.

It took Martha Purdy two years to accept George's proposal, but when she did, her life changed forever. Decades later, the couple moved to Ottawa. George Black became Speaker of the House of Commons, and later, Martha Black became a Member of Parliament at age 69.

The Klondike Mogul

Within days of her party's arrival in the Klondike, feisty, Irish-born entrepreneur Belinda Mulrooney began to explore retail opportunities in Canada's newest northern settlement. She partnered with three newcomers from Circle City, Alaska: a woman of questionable virtue named Esther Duffie, and two married women who had braved the trek up the icy river to Dawson City.

Belinda had brought long metal cylinders full of silks over the Chilkoot Trail. "I've been a fool," she thought bitterly, fearing that no one would buy delicate silks in such a boom-town environment. Hiding her embarrassment, Belinda opened one of the cylinders. The others greedily fingered the silk garments, and Belinda's doubts about how she would earn an income vanished.

Belinda watched prospectors' Native wives shuffle down the waterfront pathway in mukluks, short skirts and heavy workshirts. They came to the store, dashed away quickly and returned a while later, dragging their grizzled husbands. Esther Duffie would hold up a particularly exquisite item for the couples to view.

"What's that good for?" one miner shouted.

"That'll be a fine outfit when the mosquitoes get after you," laughed another.

Many of the women did not know how to wear the items their men bought. They were happy enough to own such fine fashions and to feel the silk in their hands.

"Next!" Esther would holler. "Who wants a beautiful night dress?"

Clever and beguiling, Esther manipulated the scales weighing the prospectors' gold in a way that made even Belinda blush. Esther might be merely a whore in Circle City, but she was a formidable saleswoman in Dawson. Belinda earned a 600 percent profit on the sale of her goods.

The women wanted silks; the men wanted meals. There was only one problem: a supply shortage. Belinda knew that every man with an outfit was a potential restaurant customer. She proposed an offer few men could refuse. If they gave her their food, they would receive cash or credit at her new restaurant. Most of the men hated cooking, so the restaurant's inventory swelled. In the land of the midnight sun, Belinda's restaurant did a roaring trade 24 hours a day.

With the profits, Belinda bought lots on Front Street, opposite the Yukon River. She dismantled river rafts and turned them into money-making riverfront cabins. After visiting the creeks, Belinda developed an idea that had the miners rolling with mirth: she decided to build a hotel not far from where Bonanza and Eldorado creeks diverged. The laughing stopped when the newly finished, two-storey Grand Forks Hotel quickly filled with tenants. Before long, a town had sprung up around the establishment. Belinda's dream, however, was to build a hotel in Dawson City. She would call the three-storey structure "The Fairview."

Others, including prospector-millionaire Alex McDonald, Belinda's rival and partner, shook their heads. "Alex and . . . Joe Barrette don't want you to try and build that hotel," Grand Forks Hotel manager Walter Gilmer told Belinda. "They don't feel you can make a go of it."

"I guess that's just why I'm going to build it," Belinda answered defiantly. "If they didn't say that, I wouldn't think of it."

Belinda secretly arranged a $10,000 bet that she would finish the hotel. One bet became many. Men even bet she would never be able to heat the building. They hadn't counted on her innovative "central heating" system. A large coal-oil tank was converted into a furnace. Later, she was told that men had put up as much as $100,000.

Build it she did, and she won the bets, too. The hotel was "by far the most prestigious structure now in Dawson," raved the *Nugget*. From Grand Forks, some eight kilometres away, the mining inspector declared the hotel open, making his grand announcement via a new invention called the telephone. There were speeches, food, champagne and dancing to "one perfectly equipped orchestra," as Belinda put it. It was a triumph for the mogul, who was all of 27 years old.

Belinda was more than a visionary. The tenacious woman managed to turn dreams into realities, not only for her own profit, but for the betterment of Dawson. Belinda Mulrooney's energy, influence and cash were behind amenities from hotels and sanitary water systems to telephone and fire services.

The pressure had been relentless throughout the hotel's construction. Belinda had needed building supplies, but time was the enemy. In Skagway, she told packer Joe Brooks it was imperative that he deliver supplies from the port city to Lake Bennett in just three days. He agreed and charged her premium fees for the task. Belinda concluded that if Joe could manage the delivery, it was worth the high price. She raced to Bennett to await the supplies. An employee hurried after Belinda, telling her that Joe Brooks had dumped her supplies at the summit of the pass! Saloon-keeper Bill

McPhee had offered the packer more money to move his whisky to the Bennett steamboats. Belinda was enraged.

Belinda and her employee rode up to the summit, hired a bunch of tough men on the trail and rode down past the NWMP post into American territory. There, they could ambush Joe and his boys without running afoul of Canadian law. As Joe's mule train ambled up, loaded with Bill McPhee's supplies, Belinda trotted into the centre of the trail. She calmly told the foreman she wouldn't budge until he had read one specific clause of her contract with Brooks. The clause stated she could take possession of Joe Brooks' pack-train mules at any time if the conditions of the contract were not met.

"We're not bothered with a contract, woman," the fore-man laughed, "You'll have a hell of a chance taking this pack train."

It seemed like a standoff, but Belinda was prepared. She had every intention of enforcing the clause. "Well, old man," Belinda smiled, urging her horse up to the foreman's, "I hate to do it, but I must." Suddenly, the foreman was looking down at the barrel of Belinda's revolver, which was prodding him painfully beneath his belt. "You better get off," Belinda warned him. The foreman dismounted.

Actually, Belinda felt she was doing the fellow a favour. "I only pulled the gun on him to give him a decent excuse for giving up the mules," she confessed. "A man had to have a decent excuse in Skagway. Of course, my men took the foreman and messed him up enough to make him feel it was a real holdup."

Belinda's gang took the mules, unloaded Bill McPhee's liquor, loaded up her supplies and took the foreman in tow. Then she offered Joe Brooks' men jobs, which they eagerly accepted. "Brooks' crew thought it was all a wonderful joke on him," Belinda recalled. To inflame their former boss even further, the men gave Belinda Joe's horse. "Everyone on the trail knew Brooks' pinto," Belinda laughed later. "Said I might as well have it. That horse was the swellest little animal I ever knew."

In the summer of 1898, at the height of the gold rush, a stocky man of medium height, proud bearing and cultured, perhaps even foppish mannerisms arrived in Dawson City. He was accompanied by a valet, of all things, and the two men immediately booked rooms in the best hotel in town, Mulrooney's Fairview. This was no prospector; this was Charles Eugene Carbonneau. The newcomer told others he was a representative of a French winery. While that may have been true, he wasn't in Dawson to market wine. He was there on behalf of a consortium of English investors to purchase mining claims.

Within days of his arrival, Carbonneau met Belinda Mulrooney. The occasion was less than auspicious: she walked in while he was arguing with her hotel manager about the cost of a bottle of wine. When she offered to pay for it, he reversed his position and insisted on paying for what she called "that darn little bottle" himself. Carbonneau's business card stated he was a count. Belinda was miffed by the title. She had no patience with people who put on airs and let him know it. He hastily snatched the card from her sight.

A French count? Others were doubtful; the rumours began. A claims foreman on the Eldorado thought he remembered Carbonneau as a Montreal barber. One of the owners of the *Klondike Nugget* heard from a man on the trail that Carbonneau had been a Montreal cook. A shocking story from the trail fuelled the rumour mill. Anxious to set a winter travelling record from Skagway to Dawson, the count had whipped his sled team furiously, leaving "dead and dying dogs behind him," the *Seattle Post-Intelligencer* reported. "Half a dozen dogs . . . almost dead from exhaustion, left alone to freeze and starve." No self-respecting sourdough could countenance such heartlessness. Suspicion gave way to animosity.

Belinda Mulrooney wrote off the rumours to petty jealousy. What impressed her more was that Carbonneau was a "dashing sort of chap in his good clothes." She admitted she found his "conversation restful and interesting." And his gifts kept coming.

As the most successful businesswoman in the Klondike (Martha Purdy would make her fortune three years later), Belinda Mulrooney was in a class by herself. Who might she choose as a suitable husband? Certainly not a typical grubby prospector. The question was important; the years were flying by and Belinda Mulrooney wanted children. Her friends suspected as much, just as they also suspected that what Carbonneau wanted was Belinda's money.

Belinda Mulrooney may have had a genius for business, but she was naive about affairs of the heart. After Carbonneau proposed, even the priest advised against the marriage. Some friends refused to attend the ceremony. The wedding went ahead anyway, one of the most lavish nuptials staged in gold-rush Dawson.

As the couple's wealth increased and their mine holdings grew, they spent winters in Paris and summers in the Klondike, and later, in Fairbanks, Alaska, where Belinda founded a bank. However, it was finally obvious even to Belinda that the count loved her money more than he loved her. In 1906, still childless, Belinda divorced Carbonneau. Thirteen years later, after being charged in a railroad swindle, Carbonneau was found dead in his French prison cell.

Belinda Mulrooney retired to Carbonneau Castle, her turreted, two-storey faux-stone home set in 20 acres of Yakima, Washington, orchards. By 1920, her Yukon and Alaska fortunes dwindling away, Belinda was renting the home out to meet expenses. In 1943, the 71-year-old former Klondike mogul donned a hard hat to help build minesweepers for Associated Ship Builders. "Well, why not?" she told an interviewer in her typical, no-nonsense style. "I've really worked all my life and this is certainly no time to be idle. We've got a war to win."

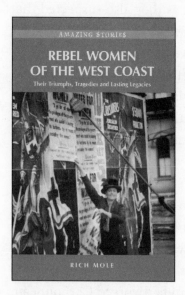

Rebel Women of the West Coast

Their Triumphs, Tragedies and Lasting Legacies

Rich Mole

print ISBN 978-1-926613-28-4
ebook ISBN 978-1-926936-28-4

Here are the stories of West Coast women whose nonconformist beliefs and actions made them rebels in society's eyes. Pioneer Catherine Schubert faced danger and starvation on her journey west. Abigail Scott Duniway endured poverty and scathing criticism during her decades-long fight for women's suffrage. Sarah McLachlan changed the face of contemporary music with her unprecedented all-female music festival Lilith Fair. These vivid biographies profile celebrated and controversial women from British Columbia, Washington and Oregon whose demands for equality and respect shaped the society we live in today.

Visit heritagehouse.ca to see the entire list of books in this series.